D0616969

James Mackay

AIRMAILS
1870-1970

B. T. Batsford Ltd London

First published 1971
© James Mackay 1971

Printed in Great Britain by
Northumberland Press Ltd, Gateshead, Co. Durham
and bound by Richard Clay (The Chaucer Press) Ltd,
Bungay, Suffolk for the publishers
B. T. Batsford Ltd,
4 Fitzhardinge Street, London W1

7134 0380 2

For Margaret and Keith

Contents

Illustrations

Preface

With the exception of a few experiments of a private nature, no airmails were flown until 1870 when the sieges of Metz and Paris forced the French authorities to adopt balloons and pigeons as a means of communicating between the beleaguered cities and the outside world. The *Papillons* of Metz and the *Ballon-Montés* of Paris thus constitute the world's first, government-sponsored airmails, and it is as a tribute to the centenary of those landmarks in the development of postal history that I have written this book.

I have attempted to survey the vast field of airmails over the past hundred years, to point out the significant developments when and where they occurred and to outline the way in which an idea born of sheer necessity in time of war has developed into the aerogramme or airmail letter which we take so much for granted nowadays.

In a book of these dimensions, however, it would be impossible to touch on every aspect of aerophilately. The exigencies of space have prevented me from giving as much detail to the development of the airposts of many countries and some have had to be omitted altogether. This book can be no more than a general guide and I would refer the reader to the selective bibliography at the end of the book for some of the vast literature on the subject where more detailed and exhaustive information is given.

If much of the emphasis of this book has been laid on the pioneer flights and the embryonic period in the development of the airmails this is only because the first half of the century under review witnessed the greatest developments in manned flight, the spanning of oceans and the linking of continents, and the glamour which surrounds the pioneer flights has resulted in them receiving more attention from collectors and students than the later, more prosaic period. This is not to adduce, however, that there is little of interest in more recent developments. The inauguration of new jet services and global flights is marked by souvenirs and 'first flight' covers just as much as the first tentative hops, and continuing development in aviation is reflected in the constant appearance of new material to interest the aerophilatelist.

I should like to express my thanks to the Trustees of the British Museum, for their permission to reproduce material from the Airmail Collection of the late Mrs Augustine Fitzgerald, and also to Mr Arthur Blair, Editor of *The Stamp Magazine* for carrying out the photography.

James A. Mackay

AMERSHAM, BUCKS
March, 1970

1

Forerunners of the Airmails

Although postal services in the modern sense date no further back in time than the seventeenth century various systems of communication have existed throughout the history of mankind. During the same period, moreover, man has been preoccupied with flight. From the legends of Daedalus and Icarus to the magic carpets of the Orient, from the ornithopter of Leonardo da Vinci to the rockets envisaged by Cyrano de Bergerac, men have schemed and dreamed of conquering the air and emulating the birds. In times of emergency, when it was imperative to send messages, people utilised such means as were available to them in order to send messages. To war is due many innovations, and this is particularly true of communications. Thus it is recorded that during the siege of Potidaea in the fifth century BC a traitor within the city received messages attached to the shafts of arrows shot from the besieging lines. Tiny scrolls containing messages and attached to arrows were a common method of rapid communcation over short distances where conventional, surface methods were too hazardous, and numerous examples of this expedient are found right up until fairly modern times.

The Chinese, to whom is due the credit for inventing so many things, invented the kite centuries before the advent of the Christian era. When they first used kites to carry messages is unknown, but the earliest examples of this on record took place in AD 549 when letters were despatched from a beleaguered city in this way. Incidentally the same method was used effectively in May 1807 by Admiral Cochrane, Earl of Dundonald, to transmit propaganda messages from the British lines to the French during the Napoleonic Wars. During the Peninsular Campaign Cochrane used kites to carry messages to and from towns when normal communications were interrupted by the French forces.

Undoubtedly the best-known example of aerial communications in early times was the carrier pigeon. It is difficult to say when man first discovered that the pigeon possessed homing instincts which could be exploited. Certainly the use of pigeons for this purpose is of great antiquity and, indeed, the earliest example of this bird being used to convey a message to man would be the dove which brought the olive branch to Noah as a token of God's goodwill. The Greeks, the Egyptians and the Assyrians are said to have used carrier pigeons and the Roman historian Pliny tells how Brutus, besieged by Anthony in Modena, used pigeons to carry messages to the Roman consuls.

Nearer our own time, during the siege of Leyden by the Spaniards in 1575 a message reached the city by pigeon announcing that the dikes holding back the waters of the Maas and the Ijssel were on the point of giving way. This gave the inhabitants sufficient warning to enable them to prepare rafts and boats. At the same time the will of the defenders to resist was strengthened and when the Spanish commander, Francisco de Valdes, called on the Dutch to surrender they sent back the reply that once they had made a meal of their left arms they would fight on with their right. Valdes, irritated by this retort, mounted a final assault, but the breaching of the dikes and the flooding of his positions forced him to beat a hasty retreat and raise the siege.

It is said that the immense fortune which the Rothschilds amassed at the time of the battle of Waterloo was due to their efficient intelligence service relying on carrier pigeons. By means of these birds Rothschild is reputed to have known of the defeat of the Napoleonic army three days before the news broke in London. This enabled him to buy shares on the London stock market at a comparatively low price and take a tremendous profit when the same shares rocketed after the outcome of the battle was announced. The relative speed and safety of pigeons as a means of transmitting communications made them very popular in the early years of the nineteenth century. After the development of more efficient telegraphic services, however, this method waned in popularity, although there have been several notable occasions in modern times, especially in conditions of war, when pigeons have proved their worth. These are dealt with at some length in Chapter 12.

Man's own attempts to launch himself into the air have a fascinating history in themselves but are outside the scope of this book. Suffice it to say that the late eighteenth century witnessed a tremendous upsurge of interest in practical aeronautics. A century earlier, in 1670, the Italian Jesuit, Francisco de Lana, proposed a lighter-than-air machine, to be lifted by four wafer-thin copper spheres from which the air had been pumped. His machine could never have flown since, had it been possible at that time to pump the air out of the spheres, they would immediately have been crushed by atmospheric pressure, a phenomenon with which Lana was not conversant. Another Jesuit, the Brazilian Laurenço de Gusmao, invented the *Passarola* or great sparrow in 1709 and in the same year built a miniature hot-air balloon which is said to have flown successfully in the presence of the King of Portugal and an assemblage of noblemen. His experiments were frowned on by the Inquisition and he was forced to discontinue them. The discovery of Gusmao's papers in comparatively recent times seems to indicate that he should be credited with the invention of lighter-than-air machines, rather than the French Montgolfier brothers whose first experiments with hot-air balloons took place at Avignon in November 1782. It is interesting to note that Brazil has served Gusmao better than has France the Montgolfiers. Gusmao's statue and his portrait appeared on Brazilian airmail stamps of 1929-40 while the Air Week stamp of 1944 reproduced Bernardino de Souza Pereira's painting of Gusmao demonstrating his 'Aerostat'. No stamps have so far been released by France in honour of the Montgolfier brothers, although Joseph, the elder of the two, appeared on a stamp issued by Liechtenstein in 1948 devoted to Pioneers of Flight.

The first public demonstration by Joseph and Etienne Montgolfier took place on 4 June 1783 when a large crowd gathered in the market place of Annonay to witness a flight by an unmanned balloon which, according to contemporary accounts, attained a height of 6,000 feet before descending to earth about a mile away. In August of the same year the French physicist, J. A. C. Charles, launched the first hydrogen balloon in Paris, an event witnessed by none other than Benjamin Franklin, the scientist, philosopher and Ambassador of the newly created United States. When someone commented about the balloon that it was interesting but 'what use is it?', he retorted, 'What use is a newborn baby?' The Montgolfiers demonstrated a balloon before Louis XVI and Marie Antoinette on 19 September 1783, sending aloft a sheep, a cockerel and a duck. The safe descent of these creatures proved that flying in itself was no danger to life. This led the way for the first tentative manned flights, the young Alsatian Jean-François Pilâtre de Rozier making the first tethered ascents in October 1783. The first free flight by manned balloon took place on 21 November 1783, when Pilâtre de Rozier and the Marquis d'Arlandes made a 25-minute flight extending about five miles across Paris. In the early days of ballooning controversy raged over the merits of *montgolfiers* (hot-air balloons) and *charlieres* (hydrogen balloons). In 1785 Pilâtre de Rozier tried to combine the two and produce a hydrogen balloon with a fire beneath it. Inevitably this highly explosive combination did not work, and Pilâtre paid with his life when his balloon blew up, at an altitude of 3,000 feet, while attempting a cross-Channel flight. The 150th anniversary of this gallant balloonist's death was commemorated by a French stamp of 1936, showing his profile, with a balloon in the background.

Although Napoleon perceived the military potential of balloons for reconnaissance the major drawback of these 'clouds enclosed in bags' was their intractability and capriciousness. Man had mastered the art of ascending and descending in balloons but once aloft was incapable of controlling the direction of flight. A certain disenchantment with balloons set in in the early nineteenth century, although a number of epic flights prevented ballooning from vanishing into oblivion. In 1836 Charles Green and two companions flew a distance of 480 miles from the Vauxhall Gardens in London to Weilburg in the German duchy of Nassau. One of the passengers on that occasion was Monck Mason who designed the first dirigible balloon in 1843. Mason's 44-foot model was powered by a clock-work propeller and is said to have attained a speed of six miles an hour.

During the ensuing decade there were several experiments with powered balloons, most of which never left the drawing board. It was not until 1852, however, that Henri Giffard invented a steam engine light enough and powerful enough (three horse-power) to be practicable. In the intervening years, balloons were employed (in 1849) by the Austrians to carry time bombs over the beleaguered city of Venice, though mercifully the damage done was superficial. Curiously enough, it was from Venice, then in the Austrian province of Lombardy-Venezia, that the first ideas of using balloons for postal purposes came in 1846. A leaflet published by Vincenzo Querini depicts an airship named *Aquila* (Eagle) with the caption PRIMA BARCA AEROPOSTALE (First Aeropostal Ship). The power for this fantastic dirigible was to be provided by means of gigantic paddles manipulated by a crew in a gondola slung below the balloon. According to the designer's specifications this balloon had a capacity of 27,000 cubic feet of gas and measured 160 feet in length. The leaflet stated that the maiden voyage of this balloon took place 'not long ago, with enormous success', but no record of it—other than this brochure—can be found.

Optimistically the promoters of this project even listed the times of flights between various cities: from London to Paris— 5-6 hours, from London to Brussels—4-5 hours, from Vienna to Munich—5-6 hours, and from Vienna to Trieste—4-5 hours. The leaflet further stated that the balloon would transport 80-100 passengers and carry a vast payload. The date of this leaflet was 21 October 1846 and it is of remarkable historical interest, if only for the reference to postal communications at a time when even surface conveyance of mail, especially from one country to another, was still in the embryonic stage.

In 1846, during the war between the United States and Mexico, an American balloonist, John Wise, proposed the use of captive balloons for the bombardment of Vera Cruz, but the US War Department doubted the efficacy of this scheme. Wise also had a curious theory that all winds in the upper atmosphere blew from the west. History might have dismissed him as yet another harmless crank but in 1859 he decided to test his theory using his balloon *Jupiter* in an ascent from the town of La Fayette in Indiana. So confident was he regarding the flight direction the balloon would take that he made arrangements with the local post office for the carriage of mail. The following advertisement duly appeared in the local newspaper:

> All persons who wish to send their letters to their friends in the East by balloon today must deliver them at the post office previous to 12m., as the *Jupiter*'s mail closes at that hour. The letters must be addressed 'via Balloon Jupiter' added to the ordinary directions and prepaid. This mail will be conveyed by Mr Wise to the place of landing with the balloon, when it will be placed in the nearest post office for distribution.

The mail was collected by the postmaster, Thomas Wood, and endorsed PREPAID before being sealed in mailbags. This procedure is significant since it indicates that the mail flight had official—albeit only local—sanction. Wise was prudent enough not to state in his advertisement the proposed destination of the balloon, which was just as well. On 17 August 1859 he began the ascent with the mailbags in *Jupiter* and eventually reached the altitude at which he hoped his theory would work. Unfortunately not a breath of wind materialised on that sunny summer day and *Jupiter* merely drifted languorously in a southerly direction. After a flight lasting several hours Wise unloaded the mail at Crawfordsville, barely 30 miles south of La Fayette, and from there the mail was forwarded to its destination by more conventional means.

For many years the existence of flown covers from the *Jupiter* ascent were unknown and many experts even doubted the authenticity of the account. Then, in 1957, the American airmail dealer, F. W. Kessler, discovered a cover bearing the postal markings and endorsements of this flight. This is the only example which has so far come to light. In August 1959 the United States issued a seven cents airmail stamp showing the balloon *Jupiter* to mark the centenary of that historic flight.

Observation balloons were put to considerable use during the American Civil war from 1862 onwards but no attempt was made to apply them to mail carrying. One of the foreign military observers attached to the Federal Army was a German cavalry officer, Count Ferdinand von Zeppelin, whose interest in balloons was aroused at this time. Although the dirigible airships bearing his name were given a military application during the First World War it is for their demonstration flights before the war and their epic world flights after, both well documented postally, that the zeppelins will best be remembered.

Small unmanned messenger balloons were employed in 1850 during the search for the Arctic Expedition of Sir John Franklin. Small balloons were launched with a piece of slow match, about 20 feet in length, attached. To the slow match were fixed bundles of leaflets at intervals of about six inches. The match was lit when the balloon was liberated and as it burned the bundles would be set loose, to be scattered by the wind. Between 2,000 and 3,000 messages, printed on thin paper varnished for protection against the elements, were carried by each balloon. Some 50 messenger balloons were purchased by the Admiralty for the use of the relief expeditions. A demonstration of one of these balloons was given at a lecture delivered at

the London Institution on 6 February 1850 but it has not been
ascertained whether this method of leaflet dropping proved
effective in practice.

2

The Sieges of Metz and Paris

The Franco-Prussian War of 1870-1, which brought about the downfall of the House of Bonaparte and the Second Empire in France, and resulted in the unification of Germany under Prussia, was the first of the truly modern wars fought in Europe. New weapons such as quick-firing cannon and machine guns revolutionised tactics in the field, while the adroit use of an efficient railway system enabled whole armies, together with their equipment and vital supplies, to be mobilised and transported quickly from one sector to another. The balloon, which had been tried by the Union forces during the recent American Civil War and abandoned as unsatisfactory, was another factor which played an important part in the Franco-Prussian War, though not in the active military role of reconnaissance so much as in the maintenance of communications.

Soon after the commencement of hostilities in August 1870 the Germans defeated the French decisively at Weissenburg, Worth, Spicheren and Saarbrucken and within five weeks had bottled up one of the French field armies at Metz, destroyed the other at Sedan, and removed all obstacles between them and Paris. The garrison beleaguered in Metz did not surrender until 28 October. During the siege, however, attempts to maintain a link with the outside world were made and one of the methods employed were small unmanned balloons which were launched from the city carrying quantities of mail. Between 5 September and 3 October some 31 balloons were released.

The first of these consisted of 14 balloons of the Jeannel-Vidau type (1 metre in diameter), known also as 'chemists' balloons' since they were invented by military chemists. Each of these balloons carried a bundle containing 150-200 'papillons', small flimsies which were, in fact, the forerunners of today's aerogrammes. The first of these balloons left Metz

1 A rare 'papillon' from the besieged city of Metz, September 1871.
Postmarked at Neufchateau on 17 September 1870

2 Flown letter journal *Gazette des Absents*, No. 14, despatched from Paris
on 7 December 1870

3 Photograph of Nadar in the basket of a balloon. Nadar, the famous balloonist and photographer, was a pioneer of the Parisian balloon post

4 Letter bearing the very rare cachet L'AEROSTIERS NADAR-DAR-TOIS-DURUOF, 28 October 1870

on 5 September and the last on 15 September. These were followed by larger balloons (4 metres in diameter) of the Goulier-Robinson type. These balloons had a much larger payload and were capable of carrying up to 30,000 papillons. The first was despatched on 15 September and the sixteenth on 3 October. One other balloon, a 5-metre Schultz type, made an abortive flight on 20 September. Between 10 and 13 September several carrier pigeons were sent out of the city by these balloons but none ever came back. Unfortunately these unmanned balloons proved to be an easy target for the Prussian marksmen and many that were not shot down were subsequently lost. Of the few which were actually recovered by the French authorities one, the fifteenth to be despatched, was picked up at Neuchateau and the papillons carried on that flight were given the transit postmark of that place on 17 September.

The only papillon recorded complete with its original envelope is now in the British Museum and came from the Neuchateau flight. Addressed to a M. Bernier in St Etienne, it bears the Neuchateau postmark of 17 September. The envelope is endorsed DÉPÈCHE EXPÉDIÉE EN BALLON while the enclosed missive merely reads: 'Metz, le 15 7bre, 1870. Je me porte bien. S. Bernier.' A few other examples of flown papillons are known without the envelopes in which they would have been forwarded to their destination. Since they were despatched unfolded and uncovered it follows that the postmark of the place where the balloons were picked up appeared on the papillon itself. The papillons were small pieces of transparent (pelure) paper, with sufficient room for only a brief message on one side and the address on the other. They were despatched unstamped and without postmarking and the only means of authenticating these rare items would have been the postmark applied, as at Neuchateau, on the flimsy itself. Examples which are undoubtedly genuine exist without any postmark struck on arrival. As there is no positive way of guaranteeing their authenticity, however, they are of considerably less value to a collector.

The Siege of Paris

As early as 14 August, when the war was barely ten days old, the bloody defeat of the French at Borny, followed by the rout at Gravelotte, opened the way for the Prussian armies to advance on the capital. On 18 August one of the most colourful

Parisians of all time, the journalist, photographer, pioneer balloonist and publicist, Gaspard-Félix Tournachon—usually referred to by his *nom de plume* Nadar—formed the Compagnie d'Aerostiers Militaires (Company of military balloonists) with his friends Camille Dartois and Jules Duruof. This arose out of a suggestion made by Nadar to General Trochu that captive balloons could be useful for observing Prussian artillery positions. Trochu gave Nadar and his associates the necessary equipment and a detachment of Marines to assist in handling the balloons. Observation stations were set up all over Paris as the menace of the German armies became more imminent.

On 4 September Napoleon III, Emperor of the French, surrendered with his army at Sedan and on the same day the Third Republic was proclaimed in Paris, under the Government of National Defence. Under this government M. Steenackers, Deputy for Haute-Marne, was appointed Director General of Telegraphs and his immediate task was the organisation of ways and means of keeping contact between the beleaguered capital and the rest of the country. Among the many hare-brained schemes suggested to him was a telegraphic cable buried in the bed of the River Seine, to link Paris and Rouen. Another idea, actually put into practice, was to put letters in metal spheres and float them downstream beyond the Prussian lines. Few of these *boules* succeeded in eluding the Germans who shot most of them as they floated down the Seine. Many of them sank of their own accord and several are known to have been recovered in dredging operations within comparatively recent times, their contents sodden but intact!

The Balloon Posts

Several of the suggestions regarding communications involved the use of balloons. One of the eminent balloonists of prewar days, Wilfrid de Fonvielle, proposed to the Republican Postmaster-General, M. Rampont, the use of small balloons with bundles of missives attached to slow match, on the same principle as those used in the Franklin relief expedition 20 years earlier. Rampont was sceptical of this project and used it experimentally only for the carriage of leaflets and proclamations. A balloon of this sort was launched on 30 September carrying four kilogrammes of leaflets, but it fell to the ground in the Prussian lines and was captured intact.

There was, however, in Paris at the time of the investment, a number of man-carrying balloons: the *Neptune* owned by Duruof, the *Ville de Florence* of Eugene Godard (who held the appointment of Aeronaut to the Emperor Napoleon), *L'Imperial* and the *Céleste* owned by Henri Giffard, and the *Napoléon* and the *Hirondelle* belonging to Jules Godard. Plans for the construction of other balloons were entrusted to the Godard Brothers, who had their workshop at the Gare d'Orleans, and Dartois with Gabriel Yon, who established themselves at the Gare du Nord. These workshops turned out a surprisingly large number of balloons, considering the conditions of the time, and altogether 65 balloons were constructed and flown out of Paris during the four months of the siege. Customs officers, thrown out of work by the siege, were employed in the manufacture of the balloons and teams of 25 seamstresses worked on the fabric of each balloon. The average capacity of the balloons was 2,000 cubic metres and it took ten hours to inflate them. Fully inflated, the balloons had a lifting capacity of 500 kilogrammes (1,100 lb). The sum allowed by the postal administration for each balloon was originally fixed at 4,000 francs. This was later reduced to 3,000 francs to the constructor, plus 300 francs for the gas and a fee of 200 francs to the aeronaut. Of the 65 balloons flown from Paris during the siege, 18 were manned by professional pilots, 17 by volunteers and 30 by Marines. Considering the very rudimentary training which most of the pilots received the balloon project worked extremely well. Only six were captured by the enemy, while two others were blown out to sea and never seen again.

By a decree of 26 September 1870, published in the *Journal Officiel* three days later, M. Rampont laid down the conditions and postal rates for letters flown out of Paris by balloon. The maximum weight was fixed at four grammes and the postage, which had to be prepaid, was set at 20 centimes. At the same time Rampont felt that the manned balloons would not suffice for the postal traffic involved, and decided to make use also of unmanned balloons, constructed of rubberised paper and capable of carrying about 100 pounds of mail. Special postcards weighing three grammes and measuring 11 by 7 centimetres were made available for this service, the postal rate being 10 centimes to any destination in France or Algeria. Regarding the costing of mail carried by balloon it should be noted that, for an outlay of about 5,000 francs per flight, the postal authorities could despatch up to 100,000 letters which, at 20 centimes each, represented a total income of 20,000 francs.

Four days after the proclamation of the Republic, Nadar, Dartois and Duruof formed their Compagnie des Aerostiers Militaires. A week later the first Uhlans (Prussian light cavalry) were reported in the environs of Paris and by 18 September the city was completely encircled. Plans for the despatch of mail by balloon were already in hand and on the 19th Nadar's company was invoiced by Numéroteurs-Trouillet, die-sinkers and stamp-makers of Paris, for a circular handstamp at a cost of 19 francs. This handstamp, applied mainly as a cachet to the Company's correspondence, was also applied to the backs of letters handed in at the office for conveyance by balloon without going through the normal postal channels. As such it is a rare item and, regarded as the world's first airmail postmark, is consequently highly prized by collectors. The letters bearing this cachet struck in red on the reverse were entrusted personally to the balloon pilots, probably after the closure of the ordinary mails, and were posted by them at the nearest post office after descent, or at Tours, when the postal administration for unoccupied France had been evacuated. This cachet was undated and bore the legend REPUBLIQUE—FRANCAISE round the edge, with AERO-STIERS—NADAR-DARTOIS-DURUOF in four lines across the middle.

Even rarer is the large blue cachet, struck in a similar fashion, by Dartois and Yon who reformed the Company after Nadar resigned in disagreement with his fellow directors. This mark also bore the inscription REPUBLIQUE—FRANCAISE round the edge, but the centre was inscribed DARTOIS & YON—AERONAUTS DU GOUVERNEMENT. Only three examples of this cachet have so far been recorded used on covers. One, in the British Museum, is on a cover postmarked 21 January 1871, although the cachet was brought into use on 1 November 1870.

An unsuccessful trial flight was made by Gabriel Mangin in the balloon *Union* on 21 September. Nevertheless it was decided to go ahead with the project, and two days later the first mail-carrying ascent was made by Jules Duruof in the balloon *Neptune*. He took off at 8 a.m. carrying 125 kilos of mail and despatches and after a pleasant flight descended at Craconville, near Evreux, about 11 o'clock. The postal blockade had been broken and the problem of communications between Paris and the rest of the country had been solved. Between that date and 28 January 1871 some 11,000 kilos of mail estimated at over two and a half million letters, were flown out of Paris by this method and the vast majority of this mail was successfully delivered to the recipients.

The correspondence carried may be divided into several categories. The bulk of the mail consisted of folded letter sheets, so that those which have been preserved have the address and postal markings intact with the letter inside. Special letter sheets, consisting of very thin paper, were prepared with various printed formulae on the front—a space for the address, sometimes a rectangle indicating the position of the stamp, and an inscription, in various sizes and types of lettering, PAR BALLON MONTÉ (by manned balloon), in the upper left-hand corner. The earliest of these unofficial air letters began to appear about 6 October.

Although the postal announcement of 26 September had recommended the use of letter sheets, many people continued to use envelopes to enclose their letters. A comparatively few types of envelopes are known bearing the printed inscription 'Par Ballon Monté' in upper and lower case type. One of the major rarities is the special envelope used by the Editor of *Le Journal Post* and including the name of this periodical in the inscription.

The postcards used in connection with the 'free balloons' consisted initially of plain rectangles of the weight and dimensions permitted by the decree of 26 September. These were endorsed, either in manuscript or in letterpress, PAR BALLON NON MONTÉ or PAR BALLON LIBRE.

Although only the simplest kind of letter sheets and postcards were used to any extent Paris would not have been Paris had not various novelties been manufactured. They consisted of cards and letter sheets embellished with the coat of arms of the Republic and inscribed PAR BALLON MONTÉ (sheets) or PAR BALLON NON MONTÉ (cards) with the date of the decree beneath. Article 4 of the decree was quoted on the front of the postcards, announcing that the authorities retained the right to seize any card bearing information which might be useful to the enemy. A flamboyant touch was added by four slogans, in both French and German, which decorated the borders of the cards or the backs of the sheets. Both cards and sheets were printed in black on variously coloured materials. Only those letter sheets printed on blue paper have been recorded genuinely used and these are extremely rare. The other colours—green, rose, azure and lilac

—seem to have been purely fanciful, for sale to collectors. The slogans were a curious blend of pacificism and defiance: 'Only one kind of war is just and holy—a war of independence'; 'glory and conquest are crimes, defeat brings humiliation and a desire for revenge'; 'stupid people—why slaughter ourselves for the pleasure and gratification of kings?' and 'Paris defies the enemy —the whole of France is preparing—Death to the invaders!'

The need to keep the rest of the country informed of events in the capital led to the production of a number of news-sheets. Some of these, known as letter-journals, contained space for personal messages; others known simply as journals were entirely composed of printed news matter. Both types, however, were meant to be folded over like letter sheets and sent by balloon post out of Paris. Eleven different letter-journals are known to have been published and some 16 different journals during the Siege. Of the former the first to appear was *La Gazette des Absents*, published by M. Jouaust. This was also the most prolific of the letter-journals, running to 32 issues between 22 October and January. The second longest in existence was the *Dépêche-Ballon* which ran to 27 numbers. At the other extreme *La Cloche* appeared on only two occasions while *Le Montgolfier* disappeared after its inaugural issue. The journals as such consisted in the main of special airmail editions of existing newspapers and, with the exception of *Le Moniteur des Communes* (which ran to over 20 airmail issues), most of them were confined to one or two special editions. Both the letter-journals and the newspapers produced special supplements and these, if intact with the rest of the issue, are of the utmost rarity. Of particular interest are the pictures and maps produced with these supplements, giving a vivid indication of the conduct of the siege. Many of the newspapers, printed in miniature by photo-lithography on flimsy paper, were sent through the post contained in ordinary envelopes.

In addition two Press agencies, Fournier and Havas, produced daily newsletters despatched by balloon post to journalists in the provinces and abroad, and there were several circulars and announcements, either official or private, which were printed on flimsies for despatch in this manner, usually with a space for the address and the stamp on the back.

The balloon flights themselves constitute one of the most fascinating chapters in the history of aviation but space does not permit a detailed account here. The flights ranged from that of the *General Ulrich* on 18 November which travelled a distance of only 22 miles in a flight lasting eight hours 45 minutes, to the epic flight of the *Ville d'Orleans* which left Paris on 24 November and, propelled by a wind of extreme violence, came down the following day at Lifjeld in Norway, having travelled 3,142 kilometres in 14 hours (an average speed of nearly 150 m.p.h.). One of the balloons lost at sea, the *Prince*, was last sighted off the English coast near Plymouth on 28 November. The other balloon lost at sea, the *General Wallace*, came down in the Bay of Arcachon, after a flight of 780 kilometres. The only other lengthy flight also ended disastrously. The *General Chanzy* left Paris on 20 December but as a result of some perversity of the winds proceeded in the wrong direction and eventually descended 470 miles away in Bavaria, in the very heart of the enemy's territory! The majority of the balloons landed in north-western France, Belgium and Holland, though quite a few came down in Britanny and the Bordeaux region.

The Pigeon Posts

No attempt was made to fly balloons into Paris for obvious reasons. Even if it had been possible to navigate a balloon accurately in the direction of the capital Prussian gunfire and musketry would have brought the flight to an untimely end. Instead carrier pigeons were flown out of Paris by balloon and subsequently used to bring messages back to the city.

Credit for this scheme must be given to M. Segalas, husband of the poetess, Anais Segalas, who approached Steenackers on 5 September with an outline of a project to use homing pigeons for the transmission of urgent messages. Subsequently the Parisian society of pigeon-fanciers, the 'Esperance', was pressed into service. Three of the society's executive committee flew out of Paris and established pigeon launching stations at Tours where members of the Government Delegation were installed after the siege of Paris began. The earliest despatches were written out by hand on tiny flimsies which were then screwed up into minute rolls, placed inside pieces of quill and secured to the tail coverts of the birds. This laborious method entailed the use of a vast number of pigeons, all of which had to be flown out of Paris by balloon and shipped by railway to Tours.

Fortunately an eminent chemist named Barreswil hit upon

the idea of photographing the despatches, reducing them on a primitive type of microfilm, and attaching strips of film to the pigeons instead. The messages were written out in large letters on cards which were then grouped together on wooden panels about 3 feet by 2 feet 6 inches in area and photographed. Each panel was reproduced in a photograph measuring only 4 by 6 centimetres, a reduction of 1 in 300.

The tremendous saving in space which this system afforded encouraged the Delegation at Tours to extend the pigeon service to private as well as official correspondence. By a decree of 4 November it was announced that anyone resident in the Republic would be permitted to correspond with Paris by means of pigeongrams. The postal rate for these pigeongrams was very high—50 centimes for each word, the maximum number of words being fixed at 20. The messages had to be printed clearly and legibly in French. Only messages of a 'private' nature were allowed. Messages for onward transmission to Paris were handed in at post offices as if they were telegrams and forwarded expeditiously to Tours for processing and photographing.

The use of the pigeon service was extended shortly afterwards to include messages from abroad. A poster published by the British General Post Office on 16 November, for example, was headed 'Open Letters for Paris—Transmission of by Carrier Pigeons', and went on to describe the conditions and terms. The messages had to be in French and limited to 20 words; the charges consisted of 5d per word, plus 6d for registration.

A total of 302 birds was despatched to Paris during the siege. Very few of the 61 despatched after 7 January succeeded in getting through, on account of the intense cold and the foul weather conditions. Some were shot down by the Germans, others fell prey to hawks. A few which were captured alive by the enemy were permitted to fly on into Paris, after their messages had been substituted for false despatches! Various refinements were made in the photographic process, under the direction of M. Dagron, Photographer to the Government. Photomicroscopy was reduced to such a fine art that the messages were no longer visible to the naked eye; 200 despatches were printed on sheets divided into three columns. These sheets were laid out on wooden panels in groups of nine or sixteen. A single panel contained, therefore, 1,800 messages or (in the case of 16 being used) as many as 3,200. The panels were then photographed on to films measuring 38 by 60 millimetres. These films were rolled to a pin's thickness and inserted into goose or crow quills, through which a silk thread was passed to fasten it to the pigeon's tailfeathers.

As the average load for a pigeon was from 12 to 18 films, a single bird could carry up to 40,000 despatches. On arrival the films were removed by splitting open the quill. They were placed in a bath of water and ammonia until they unrolled, then dried and fixed between two panes of glass. They were then projected as lantern slides in a darkened room. At the far end of the room, seated at a table near the screen, sat four telegraphists who took down the messages in longhand. The transcribed messages were then forwarded to the addressees in the normal way.

After the war Dagron sold mounted specimens of these films as souvenirs, but examples of these framed 'pellicules' are now extremely rare. Examples of the earlier microfilmed despatches, prior to the adoption of the Dagron process, are not unknown but are of even greater rarity.

Special postal stationery headed 'Dépêche-Réponse' (Despatch-Reply) was produced in connection with the pigeon posts. These cards were sold with a 5 centimes stamp already affixed, pre-paying the cost of the card. Space was included for the words 'Oui' or 'Non' in answer to up to four questions posed by the messages flown into Paris by pigeon. The cost of sending these reply-cards by balloon out of Paris was one franc. Little use seems to have been made of this ingenious scheme and flown cards are very rare, though unused examples are comparatively plentiful.

Attempts to fly unmanned balloons from Lille in the direction of Paris were a total failure. Those which came near to Paris were promptly downed by the Germans. The mail which these 'ballonets' carried was not delivered by the Germans until the siege had been raised in January 1871.

After the war it was suggested that the coat of arms of Paris be amended to include a pigeon, but the suggestion was never implemented, although the boost to Parisian morale given by the pigeon post cannot be over-emphasised. Eugène Manuel dedicated a lengthy poem to 'Les Pigeons de la Republique'. Official response could not have been meaner. The surviving pigeons were disposed of by the Administration des Domaines for one or two francs apiece. This ingratitude was belatedly repaired in 1906 when a monument was erected in Paris to the memory of the aeronauts of the siege. This bronze group by Bartholdi shows a balloon being launched and beside it can be seen the figure of a pigeon with spread wings.

3

Lighter-than-air Machines
1871-1914

The success of the balloon posts in Paris during the siege of 1870-1 had a marked influence on the revival of ballooning and also on the despatch of mail in this way. Nevertheless, until some means could be found of steering and driving balloons, this method was doomed to be restricted to emergency cases where any landfall was better than none, or cases where the carriage of mail was purely incidental and the landfall was therefore unimportant.

Emergency flights, similar to those of the siege of Paris, were very few and far between during the ensuing 45 years. Indeed no mail flight of a serious nature by non-dirigible balloons was made in this way until the Austrians were besieged in the Galician fortress of Przemysl in the early months of the First World War, described in Chapter 5. There was, however, one occasion in this period when an attempt was made with a free balloon to make a journey hitherto regarded as too hazardous by any other means, and this flight is not without its interest to the aerophilatelist.

In 1894 the Swedish engineer, Salomon August Andrée, conceived a project for a flight over the North Pole using a free balloon of French design, capable of retaining gas for 30 days. The project was partially financed by Alfred Nobel, the explosives magnate and founder of the Nobel Prizes. After an abortive attempt in 1896 Andrée and his two companions, Nils Strindberg and Knut Fraenkel, established their base at Spitzbergen in May 1897. After numerous delays on account of bad weather the Andrée expedition finally inflated their balloon and made the ascent on 11 June 1897. With them they took a number of carrier pigeons by whom they hoped to send back messages to the Swedish newspaper *Aftonbladet* which had commissioned the exclusive story of the flight. At least one pigeongram got through to the newspaper, giving Andrée's position on 12 June and the message that all was going well. A letter attached to a buoy was subsequently jettisoned two days later and gave a somewhat fuller account of the flight. A pigeon bearing a leg ring identified as having belonged to the Andrée expedition was found some months later in Arctic Canada suffering from severe exposure but apart from that nothing was heard of the expedition till August 1930 when Norwegian explorers on White Island in Arctic Russia, some 300 miles east of Andrée's starting point, discovered the frozen remains of Andrées and his companions. From the diaries and un-developed films found on the bodies the story of the ill-fated flight was reconstructed. The balloon actually flew 400 miles to the north-east before ice forming on the bag forced their descent. They abandoned the balloon and set off across the ice in search of help but perished two and a half months later. The failure of the Andrée expedition proved conclusively that free balloons were too wayward and capricious to be utilised for serious flights. Henceforward their use was confined to stunts and exhibitions, often in connection with fairs, and on many occasions souvenir mail was carried.

Ballooning as a popular spectacle had become increasingly fashionable ever since the time of Pilâtre de Rozier. As early as 1784 Vincent Lunardi made the first ascent in England and it is interesting to note that on 15 September of that year he dropped three letters from a balloon in flight. One of these was found near the milestone on Northaw Common and was returned by the finder to Lunardi. The text of this interesting letter was later reproduced in his memoirs. It became customary practice for balloonists to drop letters or cards from their machines for finders to post back to them and numerous examples have been recorded of informal airmail of this nature.

The first attempt in Britain to carry mail by balloon on a large scale, however, was made on 6 October 1870, barely a fort-night after the inception of the Paris balloon post. On this occasion a free, unmanned balloon was launched at the Crystal Palace during a fireworks display and subsequently recovered at Acrise Farm near Folkestone, Kent. The postcards contained in the mailbag were postmarked at Hythe and reached their destination by more orthodox means on the first delivery on

8 October. Examples of these Crystal Palace balloon cards are very rare and are highly prized as the forerunners of British airmails.

The carriage of mail by manned balloons in the last 30 years of the nineteenth century was sporadic and mainly confined to exhibition flights. One of the leading balloonists of this period was the Frenchman Louis Godard, son of Jules Godard who had been closely associated with the Paris balloon posts. Louis in fact piloted *Les Etats Unis,* the third balloon to make a successful flight from the besieged city. In the 1890s Godard gave a number of exhibition flights in connection with fairs and exhibitions and several of these had quasi-philatelic commemoration. In October 1897, for example, he made balloon ascents at the Leipzig Exhibition. A souvenir postcard of the period, inscribed in French, bears his portrait and records the epic flight from Leipzig to Tarnau in Silesia, a distance of 1,665 kilometres, attaining a maximum altitude of over 10,000 feet and setting up two new world records. The flight lasted 18 hours in 'rain, storm and tempest'. Postcards were flown in this balloon, the *Aug. Polich,* and bore a violet rubber stamp inscribed in German to the effect that the postcard had been carried by the balloon and posted at the point of landing.

In the balloon *Europa* Godard made ascents in connection with the Munich Industrial Exhibition the following year. Special cards were printed and a rectangular cachet with a similar inscription was applied to flown examples. In the same year balloon flights were made at the Esposizione Generale Italiana in Turin and not only were special coloured postcards prepared but they were cancelled with a circular date-stamp inscribed STAZIONE AEREA ESP. TORINO (Aerial Station, Turin Exhibition)—the first official airmail postmark.

In Britain the great ballooning era coincided with the reign of King Edward VII and appropriately the first of the famous balloon ascents of this period was made on 9 August 1902 in connection with the Coronation celebrations. Special postcards bearing portraits of King Edward and Queen Alexandra were despatched by balloon from Beckenham in Kent. One mailbag was jettisoned near Leeds (Kent), another at Godmersham and a third near Dover. The bag dropped at Dover was not discovered for three months but eventually all the cards despatched were postmarked at the nearest post office and forwarded to the addressees. The following month specially designed and inscribed cards printed in red and blue were despatched by a free balloon from Manchester in connection with 'Life Boat Saturday'. The most spectacular flight, however, was that made by the giant double-decker balloon *Mammoth* in October 1907, sponsored by the newspaper *Daily Graphic*. Souvenir postcards were carried on this ascent from the Crystal Palace on 12 October. The *Mammoth*, piloted by the balloonist and pioneer aviator Caudron (who subsequently manufactured aeroplanes in the First World War), rose to a height of over 12,000 feet and was carried in a north-easterly direction, passing over Harwich and proceeding out across the North Sea. The following evening it made a bumpy descent (which destroyed the instruments and killed a carrier pigeon) near the village of Tosse in central Sweden. A few postcards were jettisoned shortly before the descent and subsequently were picked up and posted from Mellerud. Rather more common (though the *Mammoth* cards all rank as major rarities today) were those handed over to the post office at Tosse for postmarking. The postcards were unstamped and postage due of twopence per card had to be charged from the recipients, but nowadays a *Mammoth* flown postcard would be worth £50 or more.

Although mail-carrying balloons had some measure of success in Britain, Italy and Germany, surprisingly little attention was paid to them in France where they had originated and had been proved successful. Across the Atlantic, however, free balloons enjoyed a great deal of popularity and there are numerous instances of balloon mail from the United States in the last quarter of the nineteenth century.

Professor Samuel King, who had been ballooning since 1857, made a number of important flights in the 1870s and these were not without philatelic interest. He made ascents from Buffalo, New York, on 4 July 1874, from Cleveland, Ohio, in the following September, and from the Centennial Exhibition at Philadelphia in 1876. It has been suggested that in connection with the last flight letters were carried but none has come to light in support of this claim.

During the summer of 1877 Professor King visited Nashville, Tennessee, and planned a mail-carrying flight for which he even had a special 5 cents stamp prepared. A paragraph in the Nashville *Daily American* of 15 June 1877 reads:

Balloon Postage Stamps

We have received a stamp thus termed from Wheeler Bros., No. 20 North Cherry Street, designed by Lillard, and engraved by Mr Shively of this city. It is 1½ by 1⅜ inches, has the words BALLOON POSTAGE in straight lines at the top and bottom, and is printed in blue with a good picture of the BUFFALO in the centre. All letters left at the Signal Office will be taken up in the BUFFALO. The *American* reporter will take up a supply to put on letters he drops from the clouds.

Newspaper accounts of the flight do not actually refer to mail carried on this balloon but mention messages dropped over the side in flight. A landing was made at Gallatin, 26 miles from Nashville, where the *Buffalo* was moored for the night. The following day King, with his assistants, A. C. Ford and J. H. Andrews, made a second ascent and landed at Tailorsville. Very little is known about the mail carried on this flight, although covers are known bearing the *Buffalo* stamp in addition to ordinary American adhesives cancelled at Gallatin on 18 June. One such cover is known with a manuscript endorsement at the top: 'Anyone finding this letter please put it in the nearest Post Office.' Since the *Buffalo* descended at Gallatin it seems likely that this cover was not thrown overboard, but the fact that various appeals were published in the newspapers of the vicinity after the flight, asking for finders of letters to hand them over to the post office, indicates that this practice was carried out.

The *Buffalo* stamp was, of course, a purely private production. Nevertheless it ranks as the first adhesive airmail stamp and is now a highly prized rarity. The sheet layout is not known but a single die was used to print the stamps in rows which were upside down in relation to each other, since a few vertical *tête-bêche* pairs have been recorded.

Balloon ascents continued to be a popular feature of fairgrounds and carnivals in the United States till the early years of this century and several examples of souvenir covers or vignettes are known, though to what extent these items were actually flown is debatable. In connection with the Hudson-Fulton tercentenary celebrations of 1909 a label printed in black on yellow paper referred to a 'Fulton Flight' with the injunction 'Don't Forget.' It is probable that this label was merely intended to publicise the flight and had no aerophilatelic significance.

Dirigibles

Experiments with balloons which could be powered and steered continued throughout the latter part of the nineteenth century. Prior to the invention of the internal combustion engine no motor of sufficient lightness and power could be found for the purpose but the discoveries of Gottlieb Daimler and Karl Benz in the 1880s gave tremendous impetus to the development of a dirigible balloon.

Foremost in this field was a Württemberg cavalry general, Count Ferdinand von Zeppelin, who retired from active service in 1891 in order to devote his energies to the problem. During the 1890s his greatest rivals in this field were the Brazilian, Alberto Santos Dumont and the French Lebaudy brothers. Between 1898 and 1905 Santos Dumont produced several slim, cigar-shaped balloons powered by light engines and these aerial runabouts became a familiar sight skimming over the roof-tops of Paris. Paul and Pierre Lebaudy perfected their dirigible in 1902; it was capable of a speed of up to 30 miles per hour and the following year made several long-distance flights. None of these, however, is known to have carried mail. In France interest turned from lighter-than-air machines to heavier-than-air machines after the Wright Brothers conquered the air in 1903, and although some interest in dirigibles was shown by the United States after that date it was left largely to the Germans to develop the dirigible.

Zeppelin's first airship made its maiden flight over Lake Constance in 1900. Although he had many setbacks, with typical Teutonic thoroughness he worked steadily at the development of ever larger and more powerful airships. In 1908 he perfected the first of the really great dirigibles, the gigantic Zeppelin Z-I, but the following year it exploded and was totally destroyed by fire at Echterdingen on Lake Constance. Nothing daunted, Zeppelin immediately set to work, constructing the Z-II. Funds for the construction of the new airship were partially raised by the sale of a double postcard, with a pop-up centrepiece showing the Zeppelin in its floating hangar, while the outer side showed the nacelle after the disaster. This card was sold for a comparatively large sum, the proceeds going to the rebuilding fund. Examples of it in unused condition are very scarce and used copies are virtually unknown.

Z-II was completed and made its maiden flight on 31 July

5 The ill-fated Brazilian dirigible *Pax* (Peace) in its hangar in Paris, May 1902, shortly before it was destroyed in a crash

6 One of the two surviving leaflets dropped from the *Pax* by Augusto Severo

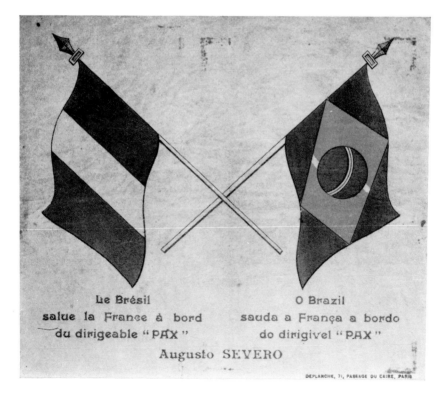

Le Brésil
salue la France à bord
du dirigeable "PAX"

O Brazil
sauda a França a bordo
do dirigivel "PAX"

Augusto SEVERO

DEPLANCHE, 71, PASSAGE DU CAIRE, PARIS

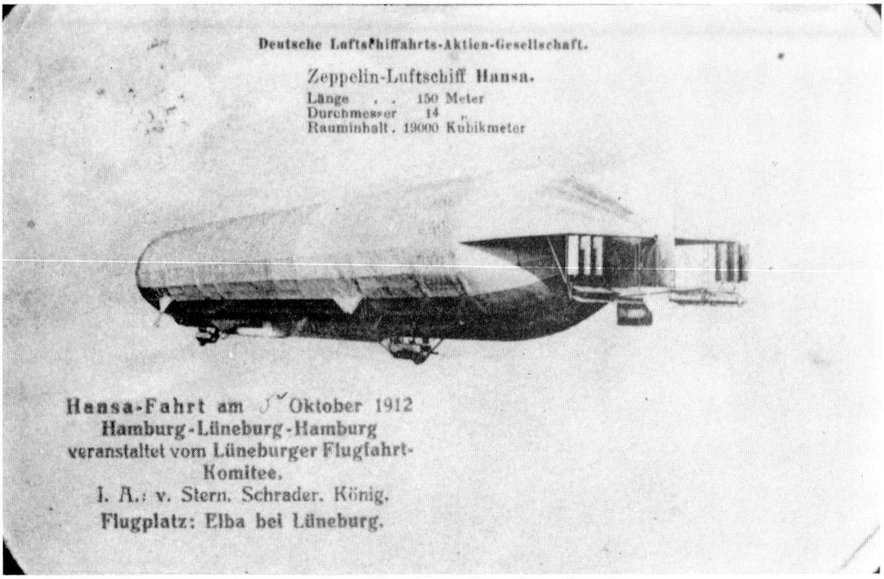

Deutsche Luftschiffahrts-Aktien-Gesellschaft.
Zeppelin-Luftschiff Hansa.
Länge . . 150 Meter
Durchmesser 14
Rauminhalt. 19000 Kubikmeter
Hansa-Fahrt am 5 Oktober 1912
Hamburg-Lüneburg-Hamburg
veranstaltet vom Lüneburger Flugfahrt-Komitee.
I. A.: v. Stern. Schrader. König.
Flugplatz: Elba bei Lüneburg.

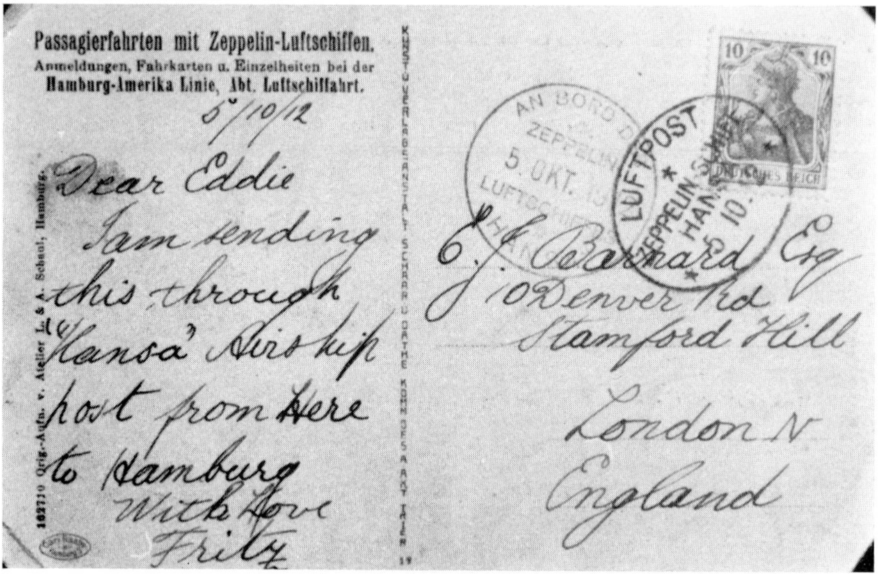

Passagierfahrten mit Zeppelin-Luftschiffen.
Anmeldungen, Fahrkarten u. Einzelheiten bei der
Hamburg-Amerika Linie, Abt. Luftschiffahrt.
5/10/12
Dear Eddie
I am sending
this through
'Hansa' Airship
post from Here
to Hamburg
With Love
Fritz
LUFTPOST
ZEPPELIN-SCHIFF HANSA
5. OKT.
6. J. Barnard Esq
10 Denver Rd
Stamford Hill
London N
England

7–8 Picture postcard of the Deutsche Luftschiffahrts Aktien Gesellschaft (German Airship Travel Company) usually known as DELAG. The picture shows the Zeppelin airship *Hansa*. This card was written by a passenger on board the *Hansa* on 5 October 1912. Note the airmail postmark and special cachet used in connection with the *Hansa* flights

1909 from Friedrichshafen to Cologne. Special cards were printed and thrown overboard during the flight. The cards bore the printed address of the Zeppelin company at Friedrichshafen and a violet cachet giving instructions to the finders to return them by posting them at the nearest post office and by filling in details as to weather, wind direction etc. Only four of these cards are believed to exist, variously postmarked at Oberturkheim, Bingen or Onadrath between 31 July and 5 August 1909. This airship made a circular flight round Cologne on 5 August and more cards, similar to the previous type but printed in blue instead of yellow, were jettisoned. Two have been recorded with the postmark of Horrem.

During 1910 and 1911 various other trips were made by Zeppelin airships, mainly the LZ-6, LZ-7 (*Deutschland*) and LZ-8 (*Ersatz-Deutschland*). Although intended primarily as passenger flights, small quantities of postcards were carried and thrown overboard. Examples of these which were subsequently found are extremely rare. In September 1911 the airship *Schwaben* made several flights from which letters or cards were dropped. The cards used on these flights had a printed inscription 'Gruss von Bord des Zeppelinluftschiffe' (Greetings on board the Zeppelin airship ...) with space for the insertion of the airship and details of the flight. A circular cachet, inscribed AN BORD DES ZEPPELIN LUFTSCHIFFES SCHWABEN with the date across the centre, was applied to these cards. This cachet is usually found in grey, but on the flight from Gotha to Düsseldorf it was struck in red. As a bonus these cards bear two dates— 7 and 12 September, the flight having been delayed by five days. Similar cachets bearing the names of the airships *Viktoria Luise*, *Hansa* and *Sachsen* were used in that period, while oval dated cachets for these three were introduced the following year.

Various souvenir postcards, showing Zeppelins in flight, were prepared in connection with these flights and were intended to be thrown overboard by passengers and crew for onward posting by the finders. In order to secure a reasonably straight fall small lead weights were attached by means of black, white and red cord (the German national colours) to one corner of the card. Presumably the finders of the cards had the commonsense to detach these weights before despatching the cards from the nearest post office. Cards with the weight still intact are unknown, with one exception now in the British Museum. This card was dropped from the Zeppelin *Viktoria Luise* over the town of Neuss on 30 May 1912. It bears the pencilled note in German, 'The honourable finder is asked kindly to place this card in the nearest letter box.' An endorsement on the card reads, 'The finder picked it up in his chicken-run, on May 31st 1912.' The message to the addressee is not without interest, reflecting the leisured times before the First World War: 'From the Zeppelin VIKTORIA LUISE we send greetings to you and your wife Luise, whilst enjoying a bottle of champagne which in the air tastes much better than on the ground!' The finder of this card forgot to detach the lead weight before posting it and as a result the Head Post Office at Düsseldorf made a surcharge of 15 pfennigs to cover the overweight!

The highlight of the summer of 1912 was the aviation fortnight staged in the Grand-Duchy of Hesse between 10 and 23 June. Flights were made during this period by the Zeppelin *Schwaben* and special airmail postmarks were used at Darmstadt, Frankfurt am Main, Mainz, Offenbach and Worms on postcards carried on these trips. Special stamps in denominations of 10, 20 and 30pf were designed by Professor Klenkens and typographed at the Imperial Printing Works in Berlin. For the flights on the last days of the fortnight the 10 and 20pf stamps were overprinted E EL P, an abbreviation now thought to mean *Ex Erste Luftpost* (from First Airmail). At the time there was much confusion in the public's mind as to the real meaning of these letters and one account states that they in fact stood for Eleanore, the Grand Duchess of Hesse, Ernst Ludwig the Grand Duke, and 'P' for the President of the Central Aviation Committee. One enterprising newspaper ran a competition on this puzzle. Anyone who guessed the names for which the initials stood and wrote them down on one of the cards sent on the particular trip advertised for their use, received a free ticket for a Zeppelin trip—or 250 marks in coin, the money to be divided in the event of several prizewinners.

Various other flights by dirigibles during the summer and autumn of 1912 were commemorated by aerophilatelic souvenirs. For the flights between Wiesbaden and Frankfurt by the airship *Viktoria Luise* from 13 to 26 October special cards with imprinted 50pf or 1 mark stamps were produced. In the same month the *Hansa* made flights between Hamburg and Luneburg and special postcards were produced.

In 1913 semi-official air stamps were issued for use on cards despatched on Zeppelin flights round Düsseldorf in April and for flights of the *Sachsen* in November of that year at Liegnitz. The last of the great pre-war airship flights which resulted in a special airmail stamp was that made by a Zeppelin between Dresden and Leipzig in May 1914. This 25pf stamp incribed FLUGPOST (Airmail) and showing an airship at the top is often found on cards bearing the oval cachet of Dresden or Leipzig airports.

No special stamps were produced for the first international airship flight, though mail carried on that occasion bore the oval date-stamp of the *Hansa*. This was a flight from Hamburg to Copenhagen on 19 September 1913. Copenhagen postmarks were applied to flown postcards on arrival and Danish stamps were added to prepay the postage to the addressees in Denmark.

It was also in 1912 that plans were first mooted for an ambitious project for the exploration of the interior of the island of New Guinea by means of a dirigible. The project was conceived by Lieutenant Paul Graetz who had earned a reputation for exploration and survey work. To him is credited the idea of using aerial photography in survey work. *The Times* of 13 January 1913 stated under the heading 'A New Airship Expedition', that:

> Lieut Graetz is making preparations for an Anglo-German Airship Expedition into New Guinea. The airship is to be built in Germany but to have an English name and to be manned by equal numbers of Germans and Englishmen. The expedition will leave Europe in October, and will be absent about two years. Its base will be a transport stationed off the New Guinea coast. In May next, Lieut Graetz expects to be able to make a preliminary flight in the Airship from Berlin to London.

Inevitable delays postponed this flight and the outbreak of the First World War soon afterwards put an end to the scheme. The sole memento of this project was a pair of stamps, printed at the Imperial Printing Works in Berlin and intended for the use of the expedition. The 2pf stamp in blue and the 1 mark in multicolour, featured the airship and the national flags of Britain and Germany. Whether they were meant to be used postally is not ascertained, but it seems that they may have been sold in Germany as a means to raising funds for the expedition. At any rate they are extremely rare, only two or three examples of each denomination being known to exist. Proofs of the stamps in other colours are believed to exist but are also of considerable rarity. The plates for these stamps were destroyed during the First World War. Contemporary (prewar) philatelic periodicals contain no reference to them and only the briefest details subsequently appeared in the German Press in the 1920s. These labels, showing the dirigible flanked by the German and British flags to symbolise the unity of the two nations, may be viewed in retrospect as one of the ironies of aerophilately, considering the use to which dirigibles were shortly afterwards put.

4

Heavier-than-air Machines
1903-1914

From the time of Leonardo da Vinci (1452-1519), who produced the ideas, to Sir George Cayley (1773-1857), who pioneered the science of aerodynamics, many philosophers, scientists and eccentrics devoted their energies to the problem of overcoming the laws of gravity and putting a machine, like a bird, into the air of its own volition. By the middle of the nineteenth century man had learned a great deal about aerial stability, lift coefficients and air currents but until a light and powerful engine could be devised to provide sufficient thrust to overcome the disadvantages of weight, these experiments were doomed to failure. Among the more practical experiments which came near to success may be mentioned the fixed-wing monoplane, powered by steam-engine, which was invented by William Henson and John Stringfellow in 1842. Together they built a model of their aerial steam carriage which made several hops of short duration under the power of twin four-bladed propellers. These short glides, made from an inclined ramp, have sometimes been hailed as the first flights by a heavier-than-air machine, though 60 years were to elapse before this could become a practical reality. It is interesting to note, however, that Henson applied in 1842 for a patent on a 'Locomotive Apparatus ... for conveying Letters, Goods, and Passengers from Place to Place through the Air.' The reference to the carriage of mail was prophetic, and it is with some justification that Henson's portrait appeared on one of the stamps issued by Liechtenstein in 1949 in honour of pioneers of flight.

Among the many pioneers of flight who have found recognition in the stamp album may be mentioned Otto Lilienthal, on stamps of Germany (1934) and West Berlin (1953), whose experiments with gliders paved the way for the early aircraft; Clement Ader (on a French stamp of 1938) whose curious bat-winged machine *Avion* of 1890 gave its name to the French word for an aeroplane; and Dr Wilhelm Kress (Austria, 1922-3), the piano-manufacturer-cum-inventor whose giant flying machine of 1898 was the first to have a petrol-driven engine.

Though both Ader and Kress came close to success, in the end it was America which claimed the privilege of conquering the air. The more scientific approach of the brothers Wilbur and Orville Wright to the problems of flight paid off when their primitive biplane made its first faltering flight on 17 December 1903. Numerous stamps have portrayed the Wright Brothers and their first biplane, including their native country (1928, 1949 and 1953), but the most interesting of these was a stamp of San Marino (1962) which also featured the ingenious lauching ramp employed to get the machine into the air.

The decade between the first flight at Kill Devil Hill, Kitty Hawk, North Carolina, and the outbreak of the First World War, saw the development of the aeroplane from an ungainly kite capable of a one-minute flight of 300 yards, to a relatively efficient machine capable of speeds up to 75 m.p.h. and a range of up to 500 miles and a maximum altitude of 10,000 feet. Many of the flying machines developed in this period were more weird than wonderful as the pioneers of aviation groped their way towards the ideal. By 1914 the aeroplane was still relatively in its infancy and its practical uses for transportation of passengers and cargo had not been developed. Nevertheless by the time of the outbreak of the First World War the aeroplane had successfully demonstrated two practical uses to which it could be put, the first for the carriage of mail and the second for reconnaissance in wartime. It was halfway through the first decade that the mail-carrying potential of aeroplanes began to be realised, while the military significance of the aeroplane was appreciated in the Italo-Turkish War of 1911 when recon-naissance flights were made in Tripoli, and in the Balkan Wars of 1912-4 when the Bulgars became the first to drop bombs on enemy targets.

Yet for much of that first decade aeroplanes continued to be regarded as toys, the novelty of which was a great attraction at fairgrounds and exhibitions, vying with free balloons for the attention of the public. Many countries have issued stamps in honour of their first aircraft. Few, however, have pandered to the thematic collector so assiduously as San Marino, whose series of 1962 with the theme of pioneer flying machines illustrates this embryonic period extremely well. The ramshackle biplane of the Wright Brothers occupied pride of place on the 1 lire stamp, while a later development on the same lines, by Ernest Archdeacon, was shown on the 2L. Towards the end of 1906 the first hops were being made in Europe. Generally speaking, official opinion regarded these pioneer aviators as dangerous lunatics and only in France, birthplace and home of the earlier ballooning craze, was there any sympathy for the new sport. The first flying school was established there and, apart from the Wright Brothers, the best aircraft designers were French. The 3L stamp showed the oddly-shaped biplane designed by the brothers, Albert and Emile Bonnet-Labranche, whose distinctive feature was the immense upper wing extending to the tail and incorporating the tail elevators. The American, Glenn Curtiss, in partnership with A. M. Herring, formed the world's first aircraft manufacturing company in 1908 and their prototype, the *June Bug* (shown on the 4L stamp) was the earliest commercial aeroplane and forerunner of the famous *Jenny* which served throughout the First World War as a trainer for military pilots and proved its worth as a mail-carrying plane in the immediate postwar years.

The greatest European airman before 1910 was the Paris-born Englishman, Henry Farman, who flew the Voisin biplane depicted on the 5L stamp. In January 1908 he made the first circular flight of one kilometre in Europe, thereby winning a prize of 50,000 francs. In October of that year he made the first cross-country flight, from Chalons to Rheims, a distance of $16\frac{1}{2}$ miles. His was the first aircraft to have wheels fitted, enabling him to fly to and from anywhere, whereas the others still used skids and required catapults to get airborne.

Louis Blériot, Leon Levasseur and Robert Esnault-Pelterie developed the first monoplane (shown on the 10L stamp) and with this machine Blériot won the *Daily Mail* prize of £1,000 by crossing the English Channel on 25 July 1909. Regrettably no mail was carried on this flight. A belated souvenir was the stamp issued by France in 1934 to commemorate the 25th anniversary of this flight and showing the Blériot monoplane over a map of the Channel. Blériot's great rival was the Englishman, Hubert Latham, who had taken up the sport of flying after his doctors had given him only a year to live! He competed against Blériot in the cross-Channel venture but his Antoinette monoplane was forced down in the sea by engine failure.

Alberto Santos Dumont, the Brazilian who had earlier acquired a reputation with his dirigible prototypes, turned to heavier than air machines in 1905 and the following year developed his strange, tail-first box kite *14-bis*, in which the pilot stood at the controls like an old-style tram-driver. In this curious machine he made the first official flight in Europe, in October 1906. In the following month he established the first world airspeed record of 25.65 m.p.h. Later he designed more conventional aircraft and favoured the monoplane shown on the 60L stamp.

As a merchant navy officer, Alliott Verdon-Roe was inspired by the flight of the albatross to design a model aircraft which won him a prize of £75. With the money he built an aeroplane at Brooklands in June 1908 and even went without food to pay for the hire of the engine. In 1909 he constructed a paper-covered triplane (shown on the 70L stamp) at Lea Marshes and became the first Briton to fly in an all-British plane. For this achievement he was prosecuted as a danger to the public safety and henceforward conducted his experiments in France. The top value of the San Marino set was devoted to an early Italian machine, a pusher biplane designed by the Turin engineer, Fascioli, in 1910. Although Italy was a comparatively late starter in the field of aviation, the Italians rapidly became one of the most air-minded nations. The Club Aviatori Roma was founded in 1909 and aviation meetings at Centocelle and Brescia were among the most popular of the pre-war airshows.

The quaint, outlandish machines built by J. C. H. Elle-hammer (Denmark), Jan Kaspar (Czechoslovakia) and Ernö Horvath (Hungary) between 1906 and 1911 have been the subject of stamps issued by these countries in recent years.

AVIATION MEETINGS

Although heavier-than-air machines were born in the United States, and were well on the way to full development in that country in the first decade of the twentieth century, it was in France that the aeroplane was greeted with the greatest enthusiasm. Wilbur and Orville Wright met with little encouragement from the authorities in America and so, in 1907, they crated up one of their biplanes and took it across the Atlantic to France where it was left, unflown, at Le Havre. In 1906 Santos Dumont made his first flights and in the course of the next two years a number of French air enthusiasts, including Louis Blériot, Esnault-Pelterie and Leon Levasseur, were experimenting with heavier-than-air machines. In August 1908 Wilbur Wright returned to France and soon won wide acclaim for his superior flying techniques which revolutionised the European aviation scene that year.

The year 1909 was notable for the establishment of the world's first flying school, at Pau in France, and for Blériot's flight across the English Channel in July. During the first week of June 1909 an Aviation Fête was held at Bar-sur-Aube. The principal motive for this fête was to exhibit different types of aircraft and although Louis Paulhan recorded, in an article written the following year, that his first flight was made on that occasion, actual flying was not the main intention of the exhibition. Yet this fête is of interest to aerophilatelists since it produced the first aviation vignette or label, showing a female allegory of Aviation seated in the clouds over the town of Bar-sur-Aube.

The following month a group of pioneer aviators met at Douai and staged the world's first Aviation Meeting. The Meeting was held on the aerodrome of Brayelle, where three years earlier Bréguet experimented unsuccessfully with a gyroplane before going on to achieve fame with fixed wing aircraft. The town of Douai took a lively interest in aviation from the very beginning and entered enthusiastically into the organisation of the Meeting at which both Paulhan and Blériot became flying celebrities. On 15 July, for example, Paulhan flew for one hour—an endurance record for that time—and finally carried out the first flight ever made from one town to another by flying from Douai to Arras. It was during this historic Meeting that Blériot established a record in circling the aerodrome, on the machine with which only a few days later he accomplished his Channel flight. From the aerophilatelic viewpoint this Meeting established several 'firsts'—the first commemorative postcard and the first vignette with designs showing aeroplanes, albeit semi-symbolic in style. The vignette featured a female figure with biplane wings fixed to her back, in flight over Douai.

The first label to feature an identifiable type of aircraft was produced in August 1909 for a meeting of hydroplanes on the shore of St Malo-les-Bains near Dunkirk. This was organised by a group of local sportsmen, encouraged by the success of the Douai Meeting, but only one entrant—Paulhan—appeared to take part. Towards the end of that month there was held a 'Grande Semaine d'Aviation' at Betheny-sur-Marne. For this occasion there was an attractive label showing a biplane over the Cathedral of Rheims. In addition there were several souvenir postcards and, for the first time, a special airfield postmark inscribed BETHENY AVIATION MARNE in a hexagonal frame. Among the pre-First World War Aviation Meetings in France for which colourful vignettes, souvenir cards and special airfield postmarks may be found were Savigny-Orge, Marseilles and Seine et Oise (1909), Cannes, Nice, Lyons, Albi, Mondorf-les-Bains (Luxembourg), Seine et Oise, Rouen, Reims, Caen, Bar-le-Duc, Nantes, Le Havre, Bordeaux and Dijon (1910), Besançon (1911), Angers and Nancy-Luneville (1912), Autun, Chatillon-sur-Seine, Issy-les-Moulineaux and Villacoublay (1913) and Nice (1914).

To what extent souvenir postcards were actually flown at these Aviation Meetings is difficult, at this distance of time, to establish. For the Nantes Aviation Meeting in August 1910, however, a small semi-official air stamp was produced and sold for 10 centimes. Out of a total printing of 192,000 stamps only 10,000 were sold and the remainder destroyed. This stamp bore the denomination '10 Cts' in the lower corners and the design was closely modelled on the celebrated Swiss stamp, known as the 'Bâle Dove', issued in 1845. Unused copies of the Nantes stamp are fairly plentiful but examples on actual postcard are now quite scarce. For the flight between Nancy and Luneville on 31 July 1912 a semi-official air stamp was produced. In this instance no doubt exists as to the nature of the stamp since it was inscribed POSTE PAR AVION NANCY. The design showed a monoplane in flight, the co-pilot rather whimsically tossing letters and cards over the side!

A total of 50,000 stamps was printed, of which some 15,000 were sold and the rest destroyed. Comparatively few stamps were actually applied to cards and covers carried on the flight from Nancy to Luneville and many of the stamps were subsequently overprinted with a red cross and used on ordinary mail after the outbreak of the First World War as fund raisers for the French Red Cross. Postcards and covers flown from Issy-les-Moulineaux to Bordeaux on 15 October 1913 bore a cachet in violet or black inscribed PAR AVION. This inscription (by aeroplane) was subsequently adopted by the Universal Postal Union for the international standard formula on airmail labels.

Germany

Early aviation in Germany was dominated by the airships of Zeppelin and Parseval and relatively little interest was shown in heavier-than-air machines before 1911. From that year onward, however, interest in aeroplanes developed rapidly and this is reflected in the aerophilately of the immediate prewar years. The first Aviation Week, on French lines, was not held until 1911 when such an event was staged at Chemnitz in May. Souvenirs of this occasion were postmarked with a black cachet inscribed CHEMNITZ—FLUGPLATZ (Flying Place) and the date. In November of that year a circular flight round Berlin and Johannisthal was commemorated by souvenir cards with an oval violet cachet inscribed BERLIN FLUGPOST VEREIN (Airmail Union) with an aeroplane depicted in the centre.

During 1912 and 1913 the aviator Hans Grade made a number of important flights on which mail was carried. On the first of these flights flown cards and covers bore the ordinary postmark of Bork dated 18 February 1912, but eight days later a special label was introduced. The frame of this label was decorated with an aerial view of the German countryside and a blank space in the centre, marked *Platz für Freimarke* (place for postage stamp), was intended for a postage stamp to be superimposed. Only 90 copies of this label were produced on glossy paper and genuine flown examples are very rare. It was later reprinted on matt paper and perforated and these labels are much more plentiful, though elusive on flown cards. Several other labels were produced for the flights by Grade between Bork and Brück in the period from March 1912 to June 1913.

A rather curious design was used for a semi-official airmail stamp issued in May 1912 in connection with a flight from Leipzig to Lindenthal which took place as part of the Margareten Volksfest (festival). This showed two winged figures in an unusual prone position and from their appearance this stamp has been nicknamed the 'Earth-scratchers'.

The most famous of all the German prewar aviation meetings was that held in the Grand Duchy of Hesse from 10 to 23 June

1912. Reference has already been made in the previous chapter to the flights of the airship *Schwaben* in connection with this event, but equally famous were the flights by the monoplane *Gelber Hund* (Yellow Dog) flown by the 'aerial postman' Lieutenant Hidessen of the Dragoon Guards. Thousands of postcards were flown by Hidessen and may be found with the special air stamps and the aviation cancellations of the Rhineland cities. On 22 June the 10 pfennig stamps were specially overprinted GELBER HUND and surcharged 1 mark in his honour. The story of how this aircraft got its name is an amusing one. One stormy day the biplane, whose wings were painted yellow, refused to rise. The quick-tempered Hidessen exclaimed angrily, 'Hatte ich dich nur oben, du gelber Hund!' (If only I had you up, you yellow dog). The constructor, Euler, overheard this remark and promptly dubbed the recalcitrant aeroplane the Gelber Hund.

Flights by aeroplanes carrying mail were made on 30 June, between Pforzheim and Karslruhe, and on 25 July, between Gotha and Erfurt. On the former occasion special postcards, inscribed ERSTE PFORZHEIMER LUFTPOST, were flown, with a circular postmark FLUGPOST PFORZHEIM—KARSLRUHE. For the Gotha flight a special 10pf air stamp was produced showing a monoplane. The inscription on this stamp alluded to the fact that the flight was carried out by personnel of the Duke Karl Edward Flying School. A lithographed 25pf stamp appeared in September 1913 for a flight between Mulhouse and Feldberg. Contrary to the usual case, this stamp is much rarer unused than on flown card.

Prince Henry of Prussia took a keen interest in the development of military aviation in prewar Germany and special Prince Henry Flights were made in 1913 and 1914 on which souvenir mails were carried. The first took the form of an aviation meeting at Giessen in May 1913, for which special labels, cachets and postcards were provided while the meeting at Darmstadt the following year was graced with an official card and an airmail postmark. The Prince Henry Flight cards were also used for a flight from Mannheim to Speyer the following day (17 May) and a special air postmark was used on that occasion also. These were the last aviation meetings and special mail flights to take place in Germany before the outbreak of the First World War. An aviation meeting, involving round flights between Breslau, Liegnitz, Posen, Konigsberg and Danzig on 20 June,

9–10 Back and front of souvenir postcard from Brescia aviation meeting, October 1909, showing an Italian biplane of the period. Note the special postmark used at the meeting

OFFIZIELLE POSTK

POSTKARTENWOCHE DER GROSSHERZOGIN 1912

Druck L. C. Wittich, Darmstadt

11 Official postcard of the 'Postcard Week of the Grand Duchess', used
in connection with flights of the *Gelber Hund* monoplane and the airships *Schwaben* and *Viktoria Luise*. Special air stamps and postmarks were
produced for the 'Luftpost am Rhein und am Main' (Airmail on the
Rhine and the Main) in June 1912

12 Pre-World War I postcard showing Engineer Schlegel, principal of
the Officers Flying School at Gotha, where many German combat
pilots received their earliest training

was cancelled at the last moment on account of the international situation (which deteriorated rapidly following the assassination of the Austrian Archduke Franz Ferdinand at Sarajevo a week later). No civil pilots took part in the Breslau Meeting and the programme was eventually carried out by the Military Air Force squadrons alone.

Italy

One of the most enthusiastic countries for pre-First World War aviation was Italy. The first exhibitions of flying by a heavier-than-air machine were given between 23 May and 18 June at Milan, Rome and Turin by the French aviator Delagrange in a Voisin biplane. Souvenir postcards inscribed ESPERIMENTO DI AVIAZIONE were produced but not flown. Nevertheless these items, especially those autographed by the pilot, are highly prized by aerophilatelists as interesting fore-runners.

Between 5 and 20 September the world's first international aviation meeting was staged at Brescia (noted on account of the fact that the first balloon ascent in Italy had taken place there in 1784). As well as an official card, showing the Italian pilot Anzani taking off in his biplane *Avis*, there was a circular cachet inscribed BRESCIA STAZIONE CIRCUITO AEREA. This memorable occasion was also honoured by a visit from King Victor Emmanuel III, while the aviators taking part included Louis Blériot and Glenn Curtiss. The aerodrome at Brescia extended over 10 kilometres in length and was rated as the largest airfield in the world at that time! During the Brescia Meeting Lieutenant Mario Calderara made a sustained flight lasting more than an hour and qualified for the first Italian air pilot's licence. Previously Italian aviators had been licensed by the French Aero Club. One of the people who took the opportunity to make a passenger flight at Brescia was the poet, Gabriele D'Annunzio. Although well on in middle age, D'Annunzio was very modern in outlook and as a result of the Brescia Meeting he became intensely air-minded, lecturing on the subject of aviation in Turin and Milan. When Italy entered the First World War D'Annunzio, at the age of 52, became one of the country's leading aces and some of his exploits are recounted in the next chapter.

In the frequency and importance of her aviation meetings Italy came a close second to France. Large gatherings were held in Palermo, Florence, Verona, Mantua, Bologna, Pescara, Milan and Turin (1910), Rome, Florence, Turin, Spezia and Rimini (1911), Milan and Siena (1912), Vercelli and Parma (1913) and Milan (1914), all of which were distinguished by special cards, labels and postmarks, of great rarity and value to collectors nowadays.

The Aviation Meeting at Milan in September-October 1910 stands out as being the first occasion when two aircraft collided in mid-air and also (as a result) of the first legal battle over the damages incurred in an air accident. Curiously enough, both litigants were Englishmen; the problems raised by this case were extremely complicated and unprecedented in legal history. But the most outstanding event of the Milan Meeting was the attempt to fly across the Alps, ending in tragedy. Nine competitors entered for this hazardous event and five were chosen: Wiencziers, Chavez, Cattaneo, Weymann and Paillet. The flight was to be made in 24 hours, and the distance covered 149 kilometres. The starting point was Brigue (Brig) in Switzerland, at an altitude of 2,800 feet and the flight involved crossing the Simplon Pass at a height of over 6,000 feet above sea level. The finishing line for the race was Domodossola on the Italian side. The route was made difficult by tortuous valleys and dangerous mountain ridges which created turbulent air conditions.

Daily observations of the speed and direction of the wind were made by Professor Mauser from the Simplon Pass, and the Meteorological Observatory at Rome sent personnel to the Italian side of the Alps to report on weather conditions. Telephone, flags and even smoke signals were used to maintain full meteorological communications and finally the flight was fixed for 18 September when the weather forecast was excellent. The Swiss authorities, however, refused to let the participants take off, since 18 September was the Anniversary of the Swiss Federation. By the following day the weather had begun to deteriorate again. Both Chavez and Weymann made attempts but were forced back by worsening weather. Weymann tried three times on the 22nd and failed. Mists were spreading and snow had begun to fall on the peaks. On Friday the 23rd the weather improved slightly and Chavez decided to make a final attempt. At 1.30 p.m. he took off, but instead of passing the Col de Monscera he was forced by adverse winds down the dangerous Gonda Valley. At Domodossola anxious crowds were watching and listening to the hum of the engine as Chavez approached.

Suddenly the engine cut out and with appalling swiftness the machine spun into the ground. Chavez died of his injuries two days later, having succeeded in crossing the Alps. The 50th anniversary of his Alpine flight was belatedly commemorated by his native country, Peru, in 1964 with a 5c stamp bearing his portrait. Other Peruvian stamps portraying Jorge Chavez appeared in 1936-7. The Italians erected a simple monument to Chavez at Domodossola. An extremely rare flown souvenir of this epic tragedy is the special postcard bearing a four-line violet cachet DOMODOSSOLA—PRIMA STAZIONE DI CONTROLLO—DELLA TRAVERSATA DEL—SEMPIONE IN AEROPLANE (First Control Station of the crossing of the Simplon in Aeroplane). Among the many flown postcards used at the Milan Meeting were some bearing small portraits of Chavez in tribute to his memory.

Great Britain

Considering the negative attitude of officialdom in Britain it is surprising that any aviation meetings should have taken place there at all in the prewar era. As it was, the few which did take place were poorly publicised and have left little in the way of distinctive souvenirs. The first of these Aviation Meetings took place at Blackpool on 3 August 1910; and on that occasion Claude Grahame-White carried despatches by aeroplane from Lytham Hall to Squire's Gate. The Air Meeting held at Lanark, Scotland, the following week, however, was far better served. Not only were there several picture postcards showing the various aviators but, exceptionally, the public were permitted to mail postcards from the Meeting postmarked with the circular date-stamp normally used for telegraphic purposes only. Postcards bearing the postmark LANARK GRAND STAND are among the greatest of British aviation rarities. A flying exhibition was staged by Grahame-White at Southport in June 1911 as part of the Coronation festivities and various attractive labels were produced to publicise the event.

The Monte Carlo Air Rally

If there was an event in the early annals of aviation which could truly be described as unique then it was the Aerial Rally at Monte Carlo in May 1914. It was organised by the Principality of Monaco, under the regulations of the International Aeronautical Federation and was designed as an aerial replica of the now-famous Car Rally which had been established three years earlier.

The *Rallye Aerien* had a forerunner at Monte Carlo in the *Meetings de Monaco* staged in the two previous years. The first meeting took place in March 1912, as an integral part of the annual Motor-Boat Exhibition, and consequently was open solely to *aeroyachts* (flying-boats) or *hydravions* (seaplanes). As well as racing over a pre-arranged circuit, the competitors were given technical tests. On this occasion the seaplanes of Henri and Maurice Farman took first and second places.

The second *Meeting de Monaco*, held on 12 April 1913, attracted a large international gathering, but the Frenchmen won all the competitive events. A highlight of this meeting was the first-ever contest for the silver cup and £1,000 cash prize offered by the air-minded yachtsman, Jacques Schneider. Of the 15 machines entered in the competition only three passed the 'ground' tests satisfactorily, and none of the pilots succeeded in completing more than half of the 500 km course round the Bay of Hercules. The seaplane races for the Schneider Trophy were a complete fiasco; the main event wore a 'come and go as you please' air, with machines stalling and capsizing all over the place.

Disappointing as the 1913 meeting was, plans were made during the ensuing year for a much more ambitious contest. It was decided to extend the 1914 meeting by staging cross-country flights, as well as seaplane races. Seven starting points were arranged, in much the same fashion as the Car Rally. These were: London (Hendon aerodrome), Paris (Buc aerodrome), Brussels (Berchem airfield), Madrid (Cuatro Vientos aerodrome), Gotha, Milan and Vienna (Aspern aerodrome). The first five routes ended at Marseilles and the other two at Genoa. Thereafter the machines were fitted with floats and flew the remaining 125 miles across the Mediterranean to Monaco. The land routes included two compulsory landing places each, and were carefully worked out so that all competitors would have to cover 677 miles. The longest single hop occurred on the Vienna route, between Budapest and Padua, and significantly no aviator attempted it.

To make the flights exactly equal, contestants starting from Paris, Gotha, Milan and Vienna had to make several circuits of their respective aerodromes immediately after take-off. The regulations also carried the proviso, 'Each competitor may start as often as he pleases.' Those who were fortunate enough to reach Monaco had to fly a competition circuit of six miles over the Bay between Monte Carlo and Cap Martin. Compulsory landings on the flights from Marseilles and Genoa had to be made at the Bay of Tamaris (Toulon) and Antibes respectively. For the lucky airmen who completed the course in the fastest time there was a prize of £1,000 and a total of £2,000 in prizes was awarded to the runners-up.

Altogether, 27 entries were received (including one Englishman) but in the event it was exclusively a contest between German and French pilots. Incidents en route to Monaco were numerous, and although the contestants had 15 days in which to get to their destination, very few actually did so. Of the 21 French pilots only six, and only one of the six German pilots, successfully completed the course.

To mark the golden jubilee of this Air Rally Monaco issued a handsome set of stamps in 1964, featuring the aircraft of the successful contestants. The 1c stamp, in a large diamond format, reproduced the souvenir postcard produced by the International Sporting Club of Monaco, showing a map of Western Europe with a view of Monte Carlo inset. It was intended that each pilot should carry about 100 of these cards. On this basis the cards ought to be comparatively plentiful, but as most pilots had to abandon the flight, the majority of the cards now in collectors' hands were never flown, or only covered part of the route by air and finished the course by road or rail. The cards were franked on the picture side by a small red stamp, inscribed MONACO 1914—RALLYE AERIEN. It depicted a seaplane in flight over the town of Monte Carlo and bore no figure of value. The label was cancelled by a small circular cachet bearing the name of the point of departure. The postmarks of the seven take-off points are of equal scarcity but that of Rome (which was a compulsory staging point on the Milan-Monaco route) is considerably rarer and all known specimens are badly blurred.

On arrival at their destination the cards were additionally stamped with a similar cachet inscribed MONACO. The only ones which may be considered to have completed the course by air are those bearing the cachets of Gotha, Brussels, Madrid and Paris. Even then, most of them were blank and unaddressed and show no signs of having gone through the post. A few, however, via the Brussels, Madrid and Paris routes, were subsequently posted from Monte Carlo and bore the contemporary Monegasque 5c stamp. These are extremely rare and greatly prized nowadays.

The six low values of Monaco's jubilee series, from 2c to 15c, featured the types of aircraft which distinguished themselves in the 1914 Rally. A curious slip appears on the 2c stamp, featuring a Farman pusher biplane with a wheeled undercarriage instead of the floats which had to be fitted for the final (maritime) lap of the race to Monaco. This was the machine favoured by Renaux and Verrier, who both successfully flew the Paris route.

Great interest was shown in England at Pierre Verrier's attempt, since he originally started out from Hendon. He made excellent time (an average speed of 52 m.p.h.) from Hendon to Calais, but on the next leg crash-landed in a meadow at Châteauneuf. It took ten days to repair his machine and on 12 April he made his second attempt, this time from Paris. On this flight, however, his biplane struck a tree at Arnet Plain, near Pezenas, and broke a wing. Fortunately Verrier was uninjured and working overtime with his mechanics he succeeded in getting the aircraft repaired in time. It was a case of 'third time lucky', for Verrier managed to reach Monaco, via Marseilles, at 12.40 p.m. on the closing day.

Bertin and Mallard both favoured the fast Niueport monoplane (one of the early pursuit planes of the First World War), depicted on the 3c stamp. Bertin set out in fine form from Paris on 1 April but, developing engine trouble, was forced to return to Buc and abandon the attempt. Malard, after several false starts, reached Monaco but broke no records on the way. Moineau, who had won the Grand Prix de Monaco at the 1913 Meeting in a Bréguet biplane, was one of the favourites in the 1914 Rally, but though he eventually completed the Paris route he was well down the list. His machine, whose distinctive feature was a large central float instead of the more conventional twin floats, was shown on the 4c stamp.

The most efficient seaplane of the period was the Morane-Saulnier monoplane, shown on the 5c stamp. Marcel Brindejonc des Moulinais left Madrid on 1 April and reached Monaco at 2.24 p.m. on the following day after a flying time of 16 hours 2 minutes. His flight was without mishap, but a squall in the Bay of Hercules gave him a bad landing, damaging the aircraft and pitching him into the sea. His ducking did nothing to daunt his high spirits at being the first competitor to arrive in Monte Carlo, and the climax to a successful day came when he was regally entertained to dinner by the Grand-Duchess Anastasia of Mecklenburg-Schwerin.

As the days of the contest wore on and only a handful of pilots staggered to the winning post, Moulinais seemed sure of winning the Grand Prix. On 6 April he set off for Milan to cover the Italian route and try to beat his existing time. Bad luck caught up with him this time and he had to make a forced landing at Pitigliano on the way to Rome.

Roland Garros, one of the earliest French aviators and a legend in his own lifetime with his epic crossing of the Mediterranean the previous September, also flew a Morane-Saulnier. Twice he had to abandon the flight from Brussels because of engine trouble, but his third attempt was not only successful but pipped Moulinais at the post. On the last day but one of the contest he flew the 677 miles from Brussels to Marseilles in a record 10 hours 10 minutes and completed the sea flight to Monaco the following morning in two and a half hours.

The progress of the Monte Carlo Air Rally was closely followed by the German Press, who saw it as a trial of strength between France and Germany. Of the two airmen who actually made a start from Gotha, only Helmut Hirth finished the course. Flying an Albatros biplane (featured on the 10c stamp) he left Gotha on 4 April and reached Marseilles 12 hours later. Near Frankfurt he had to rise to 10,000 feet to avoid snow-storms. Between Frankfurt and Lyons he battled against strong headwinds and between Lyons and Marseilles he lost his way in thick fog. Nevertheless, he beat Moulinais' time on the land route and only bad luck on the sea route robbed him of second place. He landed at Tamaris Bay as required, but on taking off again fouled his floats in fishing nets and capsized. He and his passenger were rescued but the aircraft sank.

The 15c stamp showed a Deperdussin monoplane, the machine used by the French pilot Prevost, who failed to complete the course. It was in a Deperdussin that Prevost had won the first Schneider Trophy the previous year. The close of the Rally coincided with the celebrations marking the Silver Jubilee of Prince Albert II, so that the festivities were memorable even by prewar Riviera standards. The outbreak of the First World War shortly afterwards put paid to the Car Rallies for several years and the Schneider Trophy races did not resume until 1923. Many of the young airmen, including both Garros and Moulinais, were killed in aerial combat during the war. The incredible advances in military aviation during the war took the sporting element out of cross-country flying, so the Air Rally, regrettably, was never revived.

OFFICIAL AIRMAIL FLIGHTS

Although many of the aviation meetings, air rallies and cross-country flights mentioned earlier in this chapter demonstrated that small quantities of mail could be carried, the flown cards and covers were generally of secondary importance and intended merely as records or souvenirs of the flight. In the majority of cases they were of a private nature, and although the authorities sometimes permitted a special postmark to be used, comparatively few attempts were made to transport mail by air as a regular method of communication. It was not, in fact, till 1911, that postal officials suddenly woke up to the fact that aeroplanes provided an ideal means of quick transportation of letters and postcards, if not of parcel mail.

The world's first official airmail flight was made not in Europe but in Asia. This was undertaken in connection with the United Provinces Industrial and Agricultural Exhibition, held at Allahabad in India in February 1911. It was organised by Captain (later Sir) Walter Wyndham, in cooperation with the Postmaster-General of the United Provinces, the mail of approximately 6,500 letters and postcards being flown by the French aviator H. Pequet from the Exhibition grounds to Naini Junction five miles away, on 18 February. Special, out-size postcards were produced for the occasion though a large proportion of the mail flown comprised ordinary 'commercial' letters. A large circular postmark was applied in bright magenta to the stamps on the airmail. The postmark was inscribed FIRST AERIAL POST—U P EXHIBITION ALLAHABAD with, in the centre, a pictorial representation of the Humber-Sommer biplane in flight over mountains. A few of the cards were autographed by the pilot and these are now highly prized. In 1961 India celebrated the 50th anniversary of this airmail flight by issuing a set of three stamps, featuring the famous postmark and, by contrast, a modern Boeing 707 jet-liner of Air India.

13 Regensburg Flying Day postcard, showing the special 20 pfennig air stamp produced for the occasion, October 1912

14 Postcard produced by the Sporting Club and the Aero Club of Argentina in 1912 as part of a project to raise funds for a fleet of military aircraft. A special 5 centavos stamp was issued in connection with air-mail flight

15 Egypt, 1910. Postcard bearing the cancellation of Heliopolis Aerodrome, Africa's first aviation postmark

16 Postcard in connection with Asia's first airmail—the Allahabad flight of February 1911

Great Britain

Wyndham subsequently came to England where he was responsible for organising an 'Aerial Post' as part of the festivities to mark the Coronation of King George V earlier that summer. Originally four pilots were to have taken part but one of them, C. Hubert, crashed on take-off two days after the start of the service, badly damaging his Farman biplane and breaking both legs. In the end two Blériot monoplanes and a Farman biplane were used, piloted by Clement Greswell, Gustav Hamel and E. F. Driver. The service, between London (Hendon) and Windsor commenced on 9 September 1911 and ended on the 15th. Special postcards at 6½d (including ½d postage) and envelopes at 1s 1d (including 1d postage) were produced and sold with adhesive stamps attached. Altogether 16 flights from either Windsor or Hendon were made and some 37 mailbags containing 926 pounds of correspondence were carried. Despite the large quantity of mail handled there was considerable scope for the specialist. Both cards and envelopes had a decorative vignette on the left hand side and the wording may be found with the inscriptions ... FROM LONDON TO WINDSOR or vice versa. In addition both cards and covers may be found in various colours—yellow-brown, brown, olive-green, light green or light red. Violet was reserved for cards and covers used by official personnel and such items are consequently more highly prized than the other colours. The inscription on the postmarks applied at Windsor and Hendon also varied. The various combinations of dates, flights and colours, apart from minute differences in the cards and covers, make the Coronation Aerial Post of 1911 a highly complex subject for the aerophilatelist. Six special posting boxes were used for the London-Windsor mail and the cancellations bear numerals from 1 to 6 to indicate the place of posting. Other items include newspaper wrappers (together with special flown editions) and cards with commercial advertising on them.

Though not in the category of official airmail flights there were several flights in 1912 organised by the *Daily Mail* whose proprietor, Lord Northcliffe, was extremely air-minded and later sponsored the £10,000 prize for the first Trans-Atlantic flight. In June 1912 mail was flown on behalf of the *Daily Mail* between Bath and Falmouth, via Land's End by H. Salmet. Covers were subsequently postmarked at Falmouth on 15 June. The following month Gustav Hamel made a circuit of Britain, mail being cacheted with a violet rectangular mark showing Hamel's monoplane; cards and covers are known from this flight with the postmarks of the various towns en route. In August 1912 the *Daily Mail* sponsored a Waterplane Tour of the South Coast. Special postcards were produced showing photographs of the Waterplane in flight or of Claude Grahame-White (promoter of the project) seated at the controls of the machine. These cards were marked with a rectangular cachet in violet inscribed CARRIED BY DAILY MAIL WATERPLANE in three lines of large capitals, with PROMOTED BY THE GRAHAME WHITE AVIATION CO LD underneath in smaller lettering. The cachet also depicted the biplane fitted with floats used for this tour. The postmarks of Weymouth, Portsmouth, Exmouth, Eastbourne, St Leonards, Brighton and London, among others, are known on flown cards.

In February 1913 the Robert Sinclair Tobacco Company organised a flying week at Gosforth, near Newcastle-on-Tyne. A special green label, showing a monoplane in flight was used on parcels of tobacco flown from Gosforth to Blyth, Seaham Harbour and other towns in the district. Despite the resounding success of the London-Windsor flights in 1911 the British General Post Office was curiously reluctant to develop airmail services and preferred to leave this novel method of transportation to private enterprise. In 1913 the example of the *Daily Mail* was emulated by two provincial newspapers, the *Yorkshire Evening Post* and the *Yorkshire Evening News*, both of which arranged flights carrying special editions.

United States

The United States lagged slightly behind Great Britain in the matter of official air services, the first taking place on 30 September 1911 from Garden City to Brooklyn, New York. Mail was flown in connection with the first aviation meeting to be held in the United States, the 'aerial postman' on this occasion being Earle Ovington in a Blériot monoplane. A special postmark inscribed AEROPLANE STATION was used to cancel stamps on the airmail (consisting altogether of some 43,247 pieces). Subsequently Ovington had a large rubber stamp made for use on his private correspondence; this depicted his monoplane and was inscribed round the edge 'Earle Ovington—Santa Barbara—First US Air Mail Pilot'. That this aviation meeting included mail flights at all was the outcome of the American Postmaster-General Hitchcock taking a keen interest in what was happening in England. On 27 September Hitchcock made a flight in an airship and this trip, lasting seven minutes, convinced him that aviation could play an important part in mail communications. As a result there were many flights in the United States on which mail was carried with full official blessing. Special postmarks were provided for airmail used on flights from St Louis to Chicago and at Rochester, New York (October 1911), at Fort Smith, Arkansas, Atlanta and Savannah, Georgia (November) Columbus and Albany, Georgia (December 1911), Wilmington and Los Angeles (January 1912), Oakland (February), Sacramento and Galveston (March), San Diego to Coronado and New Orleans to Baton Rouge (April), Altoona, Pennsylvania, and Milwaukee (May) and Saugus to Mass and Cicero to Elmshurst (June 1912). Thereafter the mail flights all over the United States become too numerous to mention, but all were distinguished by special postmarks and the special stationery and souvenir postcards produced in connection with them are highly collectable today. By the time the United States entered the First World War in 1917 almost 70 different airmail postmarks had been used and the nucleus of the vast network of internal airmail services had begun to take shape, receiving enormous impetus in the immediate post-war period.

Italy

Although the Italians proved to be among the most air-minded nations of the world, regular airport services were slow to develop and as late as 1925 Italy was one of the few countries in western Europe which did not have a national airline. The mountainous terrain explains the reluctance to promote internal air routes until such times as aircraft had developed sufficiently to overcome these difficulties. Nevertheless, in the period before the First World War there were several notable examples of official airmail flights. September 1911 was a momentous month for aviation history for it was then also that Italy's first official airmail took place. During an aviation meeting at Bologna on 19 September five military pilots from the new aviation school at Pardemena carried out flying tests between Venice and the Lido di Jessolo, with a return flight round by

Rimini. On the last day of the meeting a mail flight was organised by the Bologna newspaper, the *Resto del Carlino*, when Lieutenant Dal Mistro carried a bag of mail to the Lido in 1 hour 28 minutes. It is believed that all the 20 postcards carried on this flight were addressed to the same person who discreetly trickled them on to the philatelic market many years later. Very little was known of this historic flight even a decade later, but the fact that it was official is borne out by the use of an official postmark, inscribed CAMPO DI AVIAZIONE—BOLOGNA. Incidentally the officers involved in this flight were posted to North Africa the following month and on 23 October two of them, Piazzi and Moizo, made the first ever flight in wartime, during the Italo-Turkish War, when their aerial reconnaissance prevented a surprise attack near Tripoli.

On 29 and 30 October 1911 Italy's first Experimental Air Mail was held between Milan and Turin. This was a far more important landmark in the development of Italian aviation than the Lido flight of the previous month, and corresponds roughly in significance to the Coronation Aerial Post in England. The flight was organised under the auspices of the Turinese Aviation Committee and took place at Mirafiori aerodrome. Eight pilots took part on this occasion. Apart from some slight anxiety about weather conditions the start from Milan to Turin was perfect. Alberto Verona was the first pilot to take off from Milan. A second took off five minutes later but was forced to land immediately. Three other pilots subsequently took off without mishap. A vast crowd had gathered at Mirafiori to await the arrival of the aircraft. At 5.15 p.m., after a flight lasting little more than three hours, Verona's machine was sighted and circled overhead before landing gracefully. The President of the Aviation Committee, Signor Montei, congratulated Verona and presented him to the Director of Posts, to whom Verona handed a letter from the Mayor of Milan together with a bag containing postcards. Manissero and Maffeis landed shortly afterwards and handed over their mailbags. One pilot was forced to crash-land at Montrea, while the other two turned back to Milan. The return flight to Milan was made on 31 October. Three pilots, Verona, Manissero and Maffeis set out, each carrying a bag of mail. The Blériot monoplane piloted by Maffeis ran into difficulty and he was forced to return to Turin. His mailbag was later forwarded to Milan by rail, though there is no way of identifying postcards which were actually flown to their destination and those which went by more conventional means. Two official postcards were printed for this experimental mail. One bore a portrait of Verona seated in his cockpit while the other bore an allegorical subject. The postcards bore the inscription IO SERVIZIO POSTALE AEREO MILANO-TORINO TORINO-MILANO and special postmarks applied by hand read POSTA AEREO RAID AVIATORIO MILANO-TORINO-MILANO with the date at the foot, on mail from Turin, while a much simpler inscription MILANO—POSTA AEREA was used on mail from Milan.

Scandinavia

The northern countries lagged behind the rest of western Europe by only a few months in experimenting with air posts. The first mail carrying flight in Sweden took place on 3 June 1912 when the aviator Nielsen, in a B.S. monoplane, flew from Eslof to Akarp. A few postcards were carried on this flight and marked with a three line cachet SVENSK FLYGPOST—NO 2— ESLOF 1912. Despite the number shown in this cachet this flight was in fact the first. A similar cachet marked NO 3 was used on cards flown on the return trip. On 1 September of the same year the Swedish postal authorities permitted mail-carrying flights in connection with Barnens Dag (Children's Day). Three flights were made by Lieutenant Olle Dahlbeck in a Borel monoplane. A special postmark was supplied by the Post Office for the cancellation of letters and postcards, while a distinctive stamp inscribed SVERIGES FÖRSTA FLYGPOST (Sweden's first airmail) was provided by the organisers and sold at 50 ore. Some 10,000 of these stamps were printed and about half of them were actually used on mail.

Denmark's first mail flight was made on 2 September 1911 when Robert Svendsen flew across the Little Belt in his Farman biplane from Middelfart to Fredericia. He carried about 150 postcards (showing a photograph of the aeroplane) and 25 copies of the newspaper *Middelfart Avis*, which had sponsored the flight. The mailbag was tossed over the side of the plane and picked up in Fredericia where it was subsequently handed in at the post office for postmarking. This flight was quite unofficial and the souvenirs were not distinguished by any official postmark or cachet of a special nature. In July 1912 a demonstration flight took place at Hareskov in connection with the town's

Midsummer Festival. Postcards flown on this occasion bore an oval cachet inscribed FLYVEPOST NO 1 ULRICH BIRCH and a rectangular mark HØISOMMERFESTEN I HARESKOV 1912. Originally it was intended to fly the mail from Hareskov to Copenhagen but a thunderstorm forced the curtailment of the flight and the cards had to be forwarded to their destination by rail. The first actual airmail in Denmark did not take place till May 1914 when a flight between Copenhagen and Roskilde was organised on behalf of the annual children's charity day. About 3,500 special postcards were sold at 25 ore each and marked with a circular rubber stamp inscribed BESØRGET MED DANMARKS 1STE FLYVEPOST (delivered by Denmark's first airmail).

Belgium

The first airmail flight in the Low Countries took place on 2 May 1913 when the aircraft company of Brouckere-Deperdussin organised an air service between the showgrounds at Ghent and Brussels. Souvenir postcards inscribed FLYING POST—GHENT EXHIBITION in English and French were sold for 1 franc each. These cards were re-issued on 5 August for a mail flight between Ostend and Blankenberghe. A small red cachet inscribed POSTE AERIENNE BLANKENBERGHE was applied to flown cards. Very few examples of these cards have survived.

Southern Africa

The success of the Coronation Aerial Post in England inspired South Africa to organise a similar flight. One of the pilots who took part in the London to Windsor flights was Mr E. F. Driver, a South African, and on his return to his native country in October 1911 he formed the African Aviation Syndicate Ltd for the purpose of developing commercial flying in South Africa. With his partners, Compton Paterson and Captain Guy Livingstone, he arrived in Cape Town in December 1911 and began preparations of the Cape Peninsula Flying Fortnight. As a result of negotiations with the Union Postmaster-General, Sir David Graaf, permission was given for mail to be flown in connection with the Flying Fortnight. Special postcards showing a monoplane in flight over Table Mountain and inscribed FIRST SOUTH AFRICAN AERIAL POST were sold at post offices and the principal shops in Cape Town for a shilling each. On the evening of 30 December Driver took off from Kenilworth racecourse and flew to Muizenburg. Special postmarks were provided at both Kenilworth and Muizenburg and applied to flown cards. A few cards, posted at Kenilworth on 28 December, bear the erroneous date 27 December, but the vast majority of cards are dated 30 December. Two flights were made, one in each direction, and a total of 2,579 cards was carried. The return flight from Muizenburg took place on 3 January 1912.

About the same time the colonial authorities in German South West Africa became interested in the possibility of air transport and a military commission was sent out from Germany in 1913 to investigate the feasibility of the scheme. As a result of its recommendations an aerodrome was constructed at Karibib and two organisations, the Aviatik company of Mulhouse and the Aeronautical Society of Johannisthal, each sent out an aeroplane to the colony early in 1914. The Aviatik biplane was subsequently stationed at Karibib and used for transporting diamonds, while the other machine, a Roland biplane, was kept at Keetmanshoop and was entrusted with the postal service. Unfortunately the outbreak of the First World War and the invasion of German West Africa by Union troops put paid to this enterprise before it could become properly established. Nevertheless several mail-carrying flights were made in May 1914 and examples are known of covers bearing the various rubber stamps of the airmail service. Particularly prized are those items with the straight-line inscription ERSTER FLUGPOST-VERSAUCH IN DSWA. The inaugural flight was made between Swakopmund and Windhoek via Usakos and Karibib on 18 May 1914. Another rare cachet was inscribed LUFTPOST USAKOS KARIBIB I FLUGZEUG IN SUDWEST BEFÖRDERT and postmarked on 19 May.

Egypt and the Sudan

At the other end of the continent flights were made in Egypt in the same year. Egypt had shown a surprisingly early interest in flying, the first aviation week in that country having been held in February 1910 at Heliopolis near Cairo. On that occasion souvenir picture postcards posted at the meeting were cancelled with the postmark inscribed HELIOPOLIS AERODROME. The pictures shown on these cards featured well-known

Egyptian landmarks such as the Pyramids of Gizeh and the great Mosque Kait-Bey in Cairo, but primitive aeroplanes had been 'dubbed' into the background. These cards were not actually flown and it was not until exactly four years later that the first mail flights took place. Under the auspices of the Ligue Nationale Aerienne (National Air League) the French aviator Marc Pourpé made a flight from Cairo to Khartoum in the Anglo-Egyptian Sudan. Using a monoplane, in which he had recently flown from France to Morocco, Pourpé set off on 4 January 1914 and flew by various stages south to Khartoum. At Atbara he took aboard some mail and flew across the Nubian Desert to the Sudanese capital. This flight across the Sudan was a great achievement since there were no prepared landing grounds and considerable risk attached to the journey over the burning desert. Pourpé accomplished the double journey, returning safely to Cairo, via Atbara and Wadi Halfa. The journey of over 1,300 miles up the Nile was made without any mishap and Pourpé arrived in Khartoum in time for the great fête being held in honour of King George V. He gave a series of demonstration flights before Lord Kitchener, who also saw him off on the return flight to Cairo on 19 January. Pourpé reached his destination on 30 January. The few pieces of mail which he had picked up en route were marked with a large circular cachet inscribed POSTE AERIENNE CAIRE-KHARTOUM, with LNA MARC POURPÉ and the date 1913-4 in the centre. Postcards and covers were postmarked at Heliopolis on arrival and bear the date 3 February. These cards and covers are found with a combination of Sudanese and Egyptian stamps, which adds considerably to their interest.

Before leaving Egypt Marc Pourpé carried out a second airmail flight, between Cairo and Port Suez on 17 February. Although this mail flight was amply documented in newspapers and periodicals at the time, the mail carried must have been very small since no example of a flown cover came to light for almost 20 years after. An example now in the British Museum bears a three-line cachet POSTE AERIENNE SUEZ PORT S. MARC POURPÉ.

17 Postcard from South Africa's first aerial post, from Kenilworth to Muizenberg, December 1911

18 Cover carried on the first mail flight from Usakos to Karibib in German South West Africa, May 1914

Ballonpost Przemysl
1915
FELDPOSTKORRESPONDENZKARTE.

Absender
Odesilatel
Nadawca
Посилаючий
Mittente
Pošiljatelj
Pošiljač
Presentator

Dear Miske,
    This is to tell you that I have sent about 50 letters by air post. My very best wishes are sent together with this card which, I hope, will duly reach you in these dark times which are troubling our country. The passengers are carried in a little car (gondola) . With kind regards,
                          Yours sincerely, Erno.
    I trust you may receive this card.
Przemysl.

19 Austrian field-postcard flown by balloon from the beleaguered town of Przemysl in Galicia during the epic siege of 1914–15. The card bears the cachet of the balloon post and military censor marking

20 Postcard flown across the Adriatic, 1 January 1919, by the Italian Military Postal service. The card bears the special airmail postmark of Pola

5

The First World War

We have already seen how the exigencies of war gave tremendous impetus to the development of airmails, with the pigeon posts and balloon despatches of the sieges of Metz and Paris. In the period of over 40 years which elapsed between the Franco-Prussian War and the First World War only tentative moves were made towards the transmission of mail by air and it was not until the outbreak of the Great War itself that this mode of mail conveyance received great stimulus.

The Siege of Przemysl

Once again the earliest use of airmail resulted from a siege which, like that of Paris in 1870, ranks as one of the greatest in military history. Indeed, in length of time the siege of Przemysl in Galicia stands third, after the sieges of Paris (142 days) and Adrianople (137 days), the town holding out against Russian onslaughts for 136 days. The town of Przemysl on the River San was of immense strategic importance to the Austrians in their control over Galicia which they had taken from Poland in the eighteenth century. The war fever of the middle 1850s, at the time of the Crimean War, induced the Austrians to fortify the town heavily to resist any possible attack from Russia. Altogether 20 forts were constructed round the city at intervals of a kilometre.

During the First World War Przemysl was twice besieged by the Russians. The first siege came shortly after the Russians defeated the Austrians at Lvov (Lemberg) in the opening phase of the Galician campaign in the autumn of 1914. On that occasion Przemysl was under attack for a mere three weeks (19 September to 10 October), being relieved by the German advance into central Poland. The Russians fell back but continued to bombard the city. When the German right wing was checked on the outskirts of Warsaw and the Austrians were halted in southern Poland and central Galicia the Russians counter-attacked and by 5 November Przemysl was under siege once more.

An Austrian communiqué of 8 January 1915 announced that 'the postal traffic [of Przemysl] is carried out, weather permitting, by means of aeroplanes'. No detailed statistics of the postal services by air during the siege have been preserved, but in addition to aeroplanes manned balloons were used to ferry mail and despatches out of the city. On 19 March a last desperate sortie was made from the besieged town and on the same day an aeroplane and three balloons left Przemysl. The wind veered and carried the balloons northwards, landing them at Sokal, Brest Litovsk and Kamenetgletovsk in Poland, where they and their crews were captured. The aeroplane, however, succeeded in getting through to Austrian field headquarters with a letter from the commander of Przemysl stating the desperate condition of the town and asking for instructions. No instructions were sent to Przemysl and would have been useless any way since the town's food supplies had run out. The Austrian garrison capitulated on 22 March and Przemysl fell to the Russians.

Two days after the Russian troops surrounded the city balloons and aircraft were brought into use for the transmission of mail. Covers and *Feldpost* cards may be found with postmarks between 7 November and 31 December bearing a small round cachet in black or violet showing the double eagle of Austria-Hungary in the centre and inscribed round the edge K U K FLIEGERKOMPAGNIE NO 11 (Royal and Imperial Flight company). This formation also used a straight-line unframed rubber stamp bearing its name in black or violet. The postmark found on cards or covers with these cachets was the double-ring hand-stamp of the Field Post, number 101, while items can usually be further authenticated by manuscript endorsements giving the name, rank and location of the sender.

The majority of items surviving from this siege consist of *Feldpostkorrespondenzkarte* (Field Post Correspondence Cards) which also bear the circular censor mark enclosing the numerals IX 54. Five different types of this circular mark are known to have been used from the beginning of January 1915 until the end of the siege, differing in minor details. In addition these cards bore the inscription ZENSURIERT (censored) with or without other words. Altogether seventeen different types of ZENSURIERT marking have been recorded on Przemysl siege mail.

In the early days of the siege, before the Austrians became more security conscious, various unit markings were applied to outgoing mail and several of these have a particular bearing on the airmail. One of these was a large, handsome circular cachet, with the imperial eagle in the centre and the inscription K U K FESTUNGSVERPFLEGSMAGAZIN PRZEMYSL with LUFTSCHIFFSABTEILUNG (airship troop) beneath the eagle. Another cachet had a three-line inscription in blue, FESTUNGS-BALLON ABTEILUNG NO 2 (Fortress ballon troop No 2) while another read FESTUNGSARTILLERIEREGIMENT FÜRST KINSKY NO 3) (Fortress artillery regiment of Prince Kinsky, No 3). All of these markings are extremely rare, since their use was soon suppressed to prevent mail captured by the enemy revealing the disposition of troop formations in the city.

The second phase of the airmails began on New Year's day 1915. Special fieldpost cards were printed and numbered consecutively—at first in manuscript and then by means of a stamping machine. The object of this was to ensure that each unit only sent out its quota of cards. At the same time straight-line rubber stamps inscribed FLIEGERPOST PRZEMYSL (Aeroplane Post) with the year below were applied to outgoing mail. The very first of these cachets also bore the word JÄNNER (January) with the day inserted in manuscript, but this practice was afterwards dropped and only the year was indicated. The large fully dated cachets are known in a variety of colours—in blue, black or violet, while the cards were printed on yellow, yellow-brown, lemon, buff, green or pink carton.

At the beginning of February the word JÄNNER was cut out of the cachet, but was superseded soon afterwards by a similar (though slightly shorter) cachet showing the date 1915 placed centrally. Three other types of this cachet, ranging in length from 47-59mm were subsequently used. The smallest of these, being introduced shortly before the town capitulated, is of the greatest rarity.

A similar cachet, but inscribed BALLONPOST PRZEMYSL was applied to mail despatched by balloon. This cachet is known in blue, black or violet but only on blue fieldpost cards. Some of these balloon cards have been recorded with FLIEGERPOST and unit markings on them but this usage was quite exceptional.

Although balloons were used to some extent in the outward despatch of mail only aeroplanes could be used to get letters and despatches into the fortress. Generally speaking such mail was not marked in any way to indicate that it was carried by aircraft, though it can be presumed that any items actually delivered to Przemysl in this period must have been flown in. A large cachet showing the imperial eagle was applied to mail by Flieger-kompagnie No 14 which was based at Kuschan, the destination of aircraft flying out of Przemysl, but this cachet seems to have been applied only to *outgoing* mail. Nevertheless there was a curious rectangular cachet showing an aeroplane and inscribed K U K FLIEGERPOST—FSTG. PRZEMYSL with the dates 1914 and 1915 flanking the aeroplane. This mark is known in violet or black and for many years was regarded as completely bogus since it was commonly found on faked fieldpost cards produced after the war to deceive collectors. This mystery marking is, however, recorded on genuine postcards flown into Przemysl, although it is of the greatest rarity. It must be assumed that this cachet was unofficial in character but was applied *par complaisance* to mail despatched from Kuschan to Przemysl. Examples of fieldpost cards, complete with censor markings and FLIEGERPOST PRZEMYSL straight-line stamps, are known to have been forged in the 1920s, but such items can usually be detected from comparison with authenticated cards.

Adriatic Military Seaplane Service

During the First World War the Austrian forces maintained contact with military units stationed on the eastern shores of the Adriatic Sea by means of seaplanes based at Cattaro. By means of these planes mail and supplies were brought speedily to troops occupying the more remote areas of Dalmatia, Montenegro, the Adriatic islands and northern Albania, from Pola in the north to Durazzo in the south. Mail flown out of these places bore circular rubber stamps with the coat of arms of Austria and Hungary in the centre and K U K FLUGSTÜTZ-PUNKT (royal and imperial flight station) and the name of the base round the rim. This type was used at Durz (Durazzo). Other circular cachets were inscribed SEEFLUGSTATION KUMBOR (Sea-plane station), or KUSTENFLUGSTATION SEBENICO (Coastal flying station). Straight-line cachets are recorded with the inscriptions SEEFLUGSTÜTZPUNKT (Curzola or Rogoznica). KUSTENFUGSTATION (Sebenico) or UBOOTSTATIONKOMMANDO (submarine base) Gulf of Cattaro. The seaplane headquarters at Cattaro (Kotor) also used a circular marking inscribed K U K KOMMANDO DES SEEFLIEGERKORPS. All of these cachets are extremely rare. Very occasionally cards are found with the cachets of more than one base; the Fitzgerald Collection in the British Museum has a card addressed to Roth-in-Hombak bearing the circular mark of Sebenico and the straight-line mark of Rogoznica. Another card, from the same correspondence (now in the Fitzgerald Collection), bears a dated postmark K U K MARINFLUG POLA and the date 2 June 1917, but this does not appear to have been listed by any of the handbooks or catalogues dealing with the subject.

Another of the mysterious rarities in the Fitzgerald, about which nothing is known, is a fieldpost card bearing the circular cachet of the Kriegsmarine (Imperial Navy) and a circular label embossed in white on black with the double coats of arms of Austria and Hungary and the inscription K U K SEEFLUG-STATION COSADO. This name has long since disappeared off the map but it has been discovered that a tiny island in the channel of Fasana between Brioni Maggiore and the mainland near the harbour mouth of Pola was known by this name at one time. From this small island a branch seaplane service was opened since the main base at Santa Catarina within the harbour itself was too small. No other example of the Cosada label has ever come to light, although the fact that it conforms in style and production to the embossed 'seals' used by government departments in Germany and Austria at one time, plus the fact that it is tied to the card by a rubber stamp K U K KRIEGSMARINE, guarantees its authenticity. The success of the Austrian seaplane service inspired their Italian adversaries to introduce a similar service between their bases in the Adriatic and the cachets and postmarks of this airmail are dealt with later in this chapter.

Austro-Hungarian Military Air Service

Although credit for the world's first official airmail stamps must be given to Italy (see below) the Austro-Hungarian Empire was not far behind in adopting this expedient. From the end of March 1918 onwards civilian correspondence was accepted for transmission by aeroplane between Vienna, Cracow and Lemberg. These flights were carried out by Austrian military aircraft and were subsequently extended as far as Budapest. Special airmail stamps were produced for the prepayment of the air fees. These stamps consisted of the contemporary Arms series of postage stamps overprinted FLUGPOST and surcharged in new values from 1.50 to 4 kronen. The basic stamps were printed in new colours. The denominations consisted of 1.50 Kr surcharged on 2Kr, 2.50Kr on 3Kr and the 4Kr stamp printed in grey instead of the more usual green. Numerous errors were perpetrated in the overprinting of these stamps. They are known with the surcharge omitted or, in the case of the 2.50Kr, with the overprint upside down. The stamps were initially printed on grey paper but subsequently white paper was employed. Special presentation sets of these stamps were prepared without perforations and are highly prized by collectors. These stamps on flown covers are very scarce, especially the white paper varieties which were extremely short-lived.

The service was extended to Budapest on 4 July 1918 but this operated for less than three weeks and thus flown items of this period rank among the greatest rarities in aerophilately. An air service, strictly for military traffic only, was also operated between Lemberg, Kiev and Brest-Litovsk in April 1918. Field-post cards carried on these flights were endorsed with various straight-line cachets inscribed FLIEGERKOURIERLINIE (Aeroplane Courier Line) with the name of the air station underneath. A circular stamp with the double coat of arms and the inscription FLUGSTATION KIEW was also used. All of these markings are very rare.

In connection with the Vienna-Budapest air service contemporary Hungarian stamps featuring the Parliament Buildings were overprinted REPÜLÖ POSTA (Airmail) and surcharged with new values: 1K.50 on 75 filler and 4.50K on 2K. Both stamps are known with the surcharge inverted. Between 4 and 14 July these stamps were cancelled with the ordinary Budapest postmarks but from 15 July onwards a special cancellation inscribed REPÜLÖ POSTA BUDAPEST was used. Flown covers are very scarce since the service was terminated on 24 July as a result of a series of accidents.

Germany

A similar service was introduced by the Germans in the last year of the war. Military flights were made between Berlin (Adlershof) and Cologne, with mail for troops stationed on the Western Front. Military mail flights were also made between Adlershof and Hanover. Rectangular framed cachets, inscribed LUFTPOST with the date below and the name of the airfield (either Adlershof or Cöln) at the foot, were applied to cards or covers despatched in this manner. The only other military flights of aerophilatelic significance in this period were propaganda flights made over Gotha in June 1918 when cards were dropped urging the populace to sell their gold and silver to the state.

Italy

Mention has already been made of the great Aviation Meeting at Brescia in the prewar period, when the poet Gabriele D'Annunzio became interested in flying. In the immediate prewar years D'Annunzio had been living in France but on the outbreak of war he returned to Italy to urge his fellow-countrymen to take up arms against Germany and Austria. When Italy eventually entered the war on the Allied side in 1915 D'Annunzio joined the military air service. His first flight in action came on 7 August 1915 when he flew as observer with Commandant Miraglia in a seaplane from Venice across the Adriatic to Trieste, then occupied by the Austrians. The seaplane circled the town twice. On the first circuit D'Annunzio tossed overboard tiny Italian flags and numerous postbags of waterproof canvas containing messages to the Italian citizens. On the second circuit D'Annunzio successfully dropped bombs on the Austrian arsenal. Describing the event in his memoirs the poet wrote that so clear was air and sky on that summer afternoon that he was able to catch the voices of his imprisoned brothers and the murmur of the Austrian military! The message which D'Annunzio dropped was of his own composition and read,

> Courage, brothers! Courage and endurance! Fight without respite to hasten your release. In the Trentino, in Cadore, in Carnia on the Isonzo, we are gaining ground daily. Not an effort of the enemy but will be crushed by our valour. No

impudent lies of theirs but shall collapse under our
bayonets ... The end of our martyrdom is at hand. The dawn
of our joy is imminent. From the height of these Italian wings,
guided by the valiant pilot, I fling down to you as a pledge,
this message, and my heart—D'A.

Subsequently D'Annunzio became one of Italy's leading air
aces of the First World War. His greatest exploit took place on
9 August 1918 when he flew in command of his squadron
Serenissimo (named after the Most Serene Republic of Venice)
on a daring air raid in broad daylight over Vienna. Instead of
dropping bombs as he could have done, D'Annunzio and his
squadron dropped thousands of leaflets over the Austrian
capital. The leaflets bore verses of his own composition—a
quixotic gesture typical of the man. As the German newspaper
Arbeiter Zeitung ruefully observed after the flight: 'And our
D'Annunzios—where are they? We also had poets in the early
days of the war, declaiming their verses. But none of them had
the courage to become aviators.' Very few of the tens of
thousands of leaflets dropped on that occasion appear to have
survived. It is interesting to note that the Italians continued
to use aerial leaflets for publicity or as psychological war
material during their campaigns in Abyssinia and Albania and
also on goodwill flights to Greece and Turkey in the 1920s.

Trans-Adriatic Flights

One of the forgotten campaigns of the First World War was that
fought between the Italians and Austrians in the northern
approaches to the Balkans, in what is now Albania. While the
principal Austrian base in that country was Durazzo (Durz) the
Italians operated from Valona (Vlone), just to the north of the
Straits of Otranto where the Adriatic is at its narrowest.
Communications between this beach-head and the Italian mainland were maintained by fast patrol boats operating from
Brindisi and by 1917 seaplanes were also used for this purpose.
During May and June 1917 a military air post was organised
between Brindisi and Valona using seaplanes. Mail flown from
Italy was cacheted BRINDISI POSTA AEREA while that flown in the
opposite direction bore a similar straight-line cachet VALONA
POSTA AEREA. This service was of very short duration and
consequently flown covers bearing these cachets are extremely
rare.

The following year, however, a seaplane service was re-introduced. Towards the end of the war, when the Austrians were retreating northwards and abandoning the Dalmatian coast to the Italians, the latter were faced with tremendous problems of communications. An overland route was virtually non-existent while Austrian mines in the Adriatic were a hazard to shipping. The answer to the problem was to transport men, provisions and mail by air, the routes being from Venice to Trieste and from Trieste to Pola. Early in 1919 direct flights from Venice to Pola were inaugurated and Pola, Zara and Sebenico were linked by air as well. A number of cachets were used on mail posted at the various Dalmatian towns. According to most reference works this service began on 23 November 1918 but the Fitzgerald Collection contains a postcard written from Trieste to Florence on 5 November and bearing two strikes of the Venice cachet dated 11 November. The Italians made use of captured Austrian fieldpost cards and one of these is in the collection bearing three rare postal markings: the Venice cachet of 11 November, a circular stamp DIREZIONE DEL SERVIZIO AERO-NAUTICA VENEZIA and a four-line rubber stamp AVIAZIONE MARINA POSTA AEREA TRANSADRIATICA NOVEMBRE 1918 in black. The trans-Adriatic military air service was in operation until the end of 1919 when more normal communications could be resumed by land and sea.

Italian Internal Air Services

To Italy is due the credit for having produced the world's first *official* airmail stamps in 1917. Previous issues, mainly from France and Germany, had been private or only semi-official in status but the stamps released by Italy in May and June 1917 were produced with the full authority of the postal administration for a government airmail service. Experimental mail flights had been made in the prewar period but in the spring of 1917 a postal commission investigated the possibilities of internal airmail services. This commission, headed by Augusto Righi, concluded that such a service was feasible and in May 1917 plans for mail flights linking Rome and Turin were put in hand. Details of the service were announced on 16 May and the airmail rates of postage fixed at 25 centesimi for air postcards. Special postcards were produced; those in green were published by the Philatelic Club of Turin for the Turin-Rome flight while those in black on white were printed for the return flight. The aviation company Pomilio, which supplied the aircraft, also produced an advertisement card. The 25c Express Delivery stamp was overprinted ESPERIMENTO POSTA AEREA MAGGIO 1917 TORINO-ROMA ROMA-TORINO in three lines. No fewer than 200,000 stamps were thus overprinted and unused examples are consequently quite cheap even today. Flown cards on the other hand, are of considerable rarity. Special postmarks inscribed POSTA AEREA DA TORINO A ROMA MAGGIO 1917 and POSTA AEREA ROMA TORINO were used on mail carried on the respective flights. The flights took place between 20 and 22 May, the outgoing flight (Turin to Rome) being made via Savona, Genoa and Livorno while the return flight was routed via Pisa, Genoa and Turin.

On 28 June 1917 a seaplane carrying mail flew from Naples to Palermo and back and for this occasion the 40c Express Delivery stamp was overprinted IDROVOLANTE (Hydroplane) NAPOLI-PALERMO-NAPOLI and surcharged for use as a 25c stamp. Two types of postcard were issued, one inscribed COMMEMORA-TIVA ESPERIMENTO AEREO NAPOLI while the other, produced on behalf of the Red Cross, depicted Icarus. Three arrival cachets were used, the rarest having a lined inner circle. To enable people in Rome to send mail by this flight special posting boxes were erected in the capital. A return flight, from Palermo to Naples, took place on the same day and two cachets were used on mail flown to the Italian mainland. This flight was highly successful but evidently it was felt to be unnecessary and the service was not implemented. Some 130,000 examples of the Naples-Palermo air stamp were produced so they are also relatively plentiful today, though flown postcards are quite scarce.

Several flights were made by military pilots between Terranova and Civitavecchia between April and October 1918. Only the mail flown from Terranova to Civitavecchia was cacheted with a POSTA AEREA marking, mail carried in the opposite direction being unmarked. No stamps were produced for this service and flown cards and covers are extremely scarce.

France

Considering the great interest taken in aviation in prewar France surprisingly little effort was made at mail flights during the First World War. It was not until the closing months of the war, in August 1918, that an airmail service was inaugurated. Mail was flown between Paris and St Nazaire with landing points at Le Mans and Escoublac. This was the first civil air post in France and, although short-lived, was not without interest. St Nazaire was chosen as the destination of the airmail route since it was at that time an important American military base. The greater portion of the mail carried was destined for the lower Loire region and bore no distinctive markings. Nevertheless a few items were despatched with a special two-line cachet LIGNE POSTALE AERIENNE DE PARIS À ST NAZAIRE. They included some 50 postcards from the Chamber of Deputies, together with several official letters and cards addressed to prominent persons in the St Nazaire region. The postal arrangements were entrusted to Commandant Aiguillon of the military air service and the flights were made by army biplanes. In connection with this short-lived air service was the issue of the world's first airmail labels or etiquettes as they are known to collectors. Imperforate labels, printed in black on deep magenta paper and inscribed PAR AVION, were produced for use on airmail correspondence. These etiquettes gradually spread to other countries and their use is virtually world-wide today. By a regulation of the Universal Postal Union these labels have to be inscribed PAR AVION since French is the international language for postal matters, but they are usually inscribed in one or more other languages. As a sideline to aerophilately they are collected and studied avidly.

During the war there were several mail flights between the island of Corsica and the mainland but with one exception the mail transported in this way was not marked. On 15 September 1918, however, mail flown between Nice and Calvi in Corsica was endorsed with a postal cachet in red COMMISSION INTERMINISTRIELLE DE L'AERONAUTIQUE and bore the despatch and arrival postmarks of Nice and Calvi. Only about 50 items were carried on this flight and they are consequently among the greatest rarities of French aerophilately.

During the earlier part of the war, in 1914-15, military correspondence was carried between various aerodromes and aviation units and endorsed with squadron or formation markings. Over 200 different *cachets de formation* have been recorded, and although their presence does not necessarily indicate that the mail was actually flown, they are of great interest to the aerophilatelist and military historian.

Great Britain

Between March and November 1915 official service and soldiers' mail was transported by air between Folkestone and the Western Front in Belgium; this air route was known colloquially as the King Albert Line. Covers transported by air were not given any distinctive marking but the fact that they were flown may be deduced from the postmarks applied on despatch and arrival and the addresses shown on covers and cards. During the latter part of the war this air service was vastly extended. Here again, proof of flight can only be shown in the cachets of military units and the dates and locations of field post office markings (such as those used by British units attached to French aerodromes). The 'King Albert Line' was resumed in 1917-8, but operated by Belgian aircraft flying from London to the Western Front. In the same period a regular airmail service was operated by naval seaplanes from Lake Windermere to the Isle of Man. The seaplanes were employed on anti-U-Boat patrol but the opportunity was taken to utilise them for postal work. Mail flown by this means can only be identified by the postmarks and dates on letters and cards, since no distinctive cachets were employed.

Britain made greater use of aeroplanes and balloons during the First World War for propaganda purposes. These flights, in which leaflets, news-sheets, newspapers and cards were dropped, were of two kinds—either directed against the enemy or over home territory for publicity reasons. Leaflets and newsletters written in German were dropped over the enemy lines between 1915 and 1918. Examples of these leaflets and other documents are recorded with the inscription 'By Balloon—Durch Luftballon'. Others consisted of facsimile letters from prisoners of war addressed to their kin. In some cases the recipient was requested to state where the card had been picked up, when replying to the prisoner. In this way British Intelligence hoped to discover information on weather conditions and prevailing winds. Although this data was of dubious military value the Germans were careful to confiscate most of the prisoners' cards recovered on German territory.

Much of the material dropped over Britain by the Royal Flying Corps and later the Royal Air Force consisted of leaflets advertising War Loans, Tank Weeks and Defence Bond

21 Cover carried by military aircraft on Mexico's first mail flight, July 1917. The cachet PRIMER Correo Aereo (First Airmail) is probably the largest ever used in connection with airmails

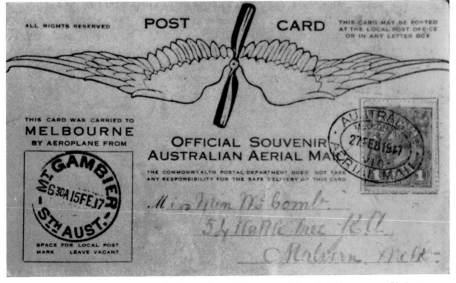

22 Australian postcard for the Mt Gambier–Melbourne flight, February 1917

23 Semi-official air stamps *1* Germany *Gelber Hund,* 1912 *2* Chile,
Figueroa, 1919 *3 Gelber Hund* with inverted overprint *4* Canada,
1918, Montreal–Toronto flight *5, 6* Germany, 1912, Bork–Brück
flights *7* Canada, 1926, London (Ont.) to London (England) flight.
Of the 100 stamps printed, 97 were affixed to mail which was lost when
the aircraft crashed in the Atlantic. One of the three surviving unused
examples

projects. An unusual leaflet was that dropped by RAF aircraft over Birmingham in September 1918 during 'Win the War Week'. The leaflets were entitled *First Message from Mars* and contained an acknowledgment of Birmingham's war efforts on behalf of the RAF.

At the end of the war a British military air service was established between Marquise near Boulogne, Valenciennes, Namur and Spa. This service was gradually extended in both directions and in March 1919 linked London to Cologne. Mail was carried by aircraft of No 120 Bomber Squadron operating from Hawkinge Aerodrome near Folkestone to Maisoncelle Aerodrome at Marquise where the mailbags were transhipped to aircraft from No 110 or No 18 Squadrons which completed the journey to Cologne. The British military airmail of June 1918 onwards was stamped with a large circular datestamp inscribed FOREIGN AIRCRAFT SERVICE—3 or a circular cachet inscribed ROYAL AIR FORCE. These markings were confined to official mail and are therefore very scarce today. The mail carried by the RAF between Folkestone and Cologne after the war bore the Army Post Office cancellation S20. Incidentally, the fiftieth anniversary of the inauguration of the Kent-Cologne mail flights was celebrated in 1969 by a special postmark used by the British Army Post Office located at the present day in Cologne.

British Commonwealth

A number of airmail flights was made during the First World War which, though not directly concerned with the prosecution of the war, had some bearing on the war effort. These flights were for publicity purposes, to raise funds for troop comforts and the Red Cross. The best known of these were made in the Union of South Africa from October to December 1918. The flights were made by Lieutenant A. H. Gearing, RAF, flying a BE 2E biplane which had been presented to the British Government by the citizens of Buenos Aires in Argentina and which was stationed throughout the latter part of the war in South Africa. Special postcards were prepared and sold for 6d each on behalf of the Red Cross. These cards bore a RAF emblem superimposed on a red cross, with the inscription MAKE YOUR SIXPENCE FLY. Souvenir envelopes, and even a special airmail edition of *The Aerial News*, were prepared in connection with the 'Our Day' flights in Cape Province in October 1918. A distinctive postmark inscribed AERIAL POST round the edge and SOUTH AFRICA with the date in the centre, was used to cancel this airmail.

Several flights were made in Australia in 1917 but these were more in the nature of experimental airmails rather than morale boosters for the war effort. An experimental flight was made between 15 and 27 February 1917 by Basil Watson, linking Mount Gambier to Melbourne, via Hamilton, Casterton and Warrnambool. Special postcards inscribed OFFICIAL SOUVENIR AUSTRALIAN AERIAL MAIL were produced and mailed to Melbourne from the various staging points on the route. On 23 November R. Graham Carey made a flight by Blériot 60 h.p. monoplane between Adelaide and Gawler. The special cards on this occasion featured draped Union Jack and Australian flags on the reverse and had a quasi-patriotic motive.

Between 15 August and 4 September 1918 several flights were made between Ottawa and Toronto in both directions under the auspices of the Aero Club of Canada. Mail was transmitted by permission of the Minister of Posts and special stamps were produced by the Aero Club to frank the airmail. These semi-official stamps, printed by the United Typewriter Company of Toronto, were of 25 cents denomination and bore the legend round all four sides THE AERO CLUB OF CANADA FIRST AERIAL MAIL SERVICE—PER ROYAL AIR FORCE 25—AUGUST 1918—25. As a tribute to the Royal Air Force whose machines carried this mail, the vignette of the stamp featured a spirited action scene between a RAF biplane and a German Zeppelin, the latter going down in flames. A few examples of this stamp are known with the flames omitted; the red colour was inserted by printing at a second operation and one row of six stamps on one sheet apparently missed this printing.

In retrospect it may seem that comparatively little use was made of aircraft for the carriage of mail during the First World War, but the enormous developments in aviation which the war stimulated were to have the greatest significance on the development of the airmails in the immediate postwar years.

6

Pioneer World Flights
1919-1930

The year after the First World War witnessed the greatest single step forward in the history of manned flight since the first faltering hops of the Wright Brothers 16 years earlier. Within months of the cessation of hostilities men succeeded not only in bridging the Atlantic but in opening up air routes from Britain to Egypt, India, the Far East and Australia. The technological advances in aeronautics during the war and the giant machines developed during that period made the great pioneer flights across the world in the early 1920s a possibility. In many cases the intrepid aviators who blazed the trail from one side of the globe to the other carried a small quantity of mail and the covers and cards from these historic flights are highly prized by collectors and aviation historians.

Trans-Atlantic Flights 1919

Such is the ambition of mankind that the first biplanes had hardly taken to the air when plans were being laid for a trans-Atlantic flight and, in fact, the first attempt was made in October 1910. Admittedly this attempt was made by a powered balloon, the *America*, and the flight was abandoned on account of bad weather conditions north of Bermuda. Nevertheless it showed that a trans-Atlantic flight was feasible, given the machine powerful enough to carry it out.

Few people have ever been more air-minded than the first Lord Northcliffe whose encouragement to aviators before the First World War included the offer of large cash prizes for the fastest flights from London to Manchester (1910) and the round Britain flight (1911). In 1913 he announced, through his newspaper, the *Daily Mail,* a prize of £10,000 for the first successful flight across the Atlantic. The offer drew forth an international, if small, response and entrants from Britain, the United States, France and Germany signified their intention of competing for the money in the summer of 1914. The American entry, using a Curtiss amphibian, was enthusiastically sponsored by the Aero Club of America as symbolising the centenary of peace between Britain and the United States.

An attempt to celebrate the peace of 1814 was shattered by the outbreak of the war of 1914 and the proposed Atlantic competition was shelved for the duration of the war. Early in 1919 the *Daily Mail* repeated its offer and by the end of March 1919 six entries had been received. Subsequently there were four late entries including one from Vickers. All the competitors, except Major Wood piloting a Short *Shiel,* planned to fly from west to east. Major Wood, however, was forced to ditch in the Atlantic off the Irish coast during a trial flight, and for various reasons most of the contestants either dropped out or were too late in finalising their arrangements. In the event only four attempts were made in the *Daily Mail* contest.

In chronological order of their arrival in Newfoundland, to make their attempt on the Atlantic, the aircraft were as follows: Sopwith *Atlantic* piloted by Harry Hawker and navigated by Lieut-Cdr Kenneth Mackenzie-Grieve; Martinsyde *Raymor* (the name being compounded from Major Raynham the pilot and Major Morgan the navigator); Handley Page V/1500 *Atlantic* with a crew of six, including Admiral Sir Mark Kerr (commander), Major Brackley (pilot) and Major Trygve Gran (navigator); and last, but by no means least, Vickers *Vimy* piloted by Captain John Alcock and navigated by Lieut Arthur Whitten-Brown.

The conditions of the contest laid down that the flight had to be non-stop between any point in Great Britain and any point in Canada, Newfoundland or the United States. This therefore ruled out a rival attempt made simultaneously by the United States Navy which organised a team of four flying boats for a flight from Newfoundland to the Azores and thence to Lisbon. Then as now, the United States provided massive logistical backing to the enterprise, with no fewer than 27 destroyers posted at strategic intervals along the route to give assistance should any of the aircraft be forced down. Only one of these flying boats completed the course, taking 12 days to do

24 Airmail Rarities *1* The world's first official airmail stamp, Italy,
May 1917 *2* The unissued Italian Levant air stamp, 1919, with
'Specimen' endorsement *3* The 'Inverted Jenny', the US 24 cents
stamp of 1918 with inverted centre *4* Bolivia 10 centavos 1924, with
inverted centre *5* Colombia 2 centavos, overprinted for the first airmail service, June 1919. Only 200 stamps were produced. The centre
stamp shows the variety seriffed '1' in the date '18' *6* France 1928,
Berthelot stamps surcharged 10 francs by authority of the French
Consul-General in New York to prepay the special fee on mail flown by
catapult aircraft from the liner *Ile de France*

25 Possibly the rarest flown cover in the world. A Martinsyde souvenir bearing both 'Hawker' and 'Martinsyde' air stamps of Newfoundland autographed by the Martinsyde navigator, Major Morgan. This cover, addressed to the Editor of the *Daily Express*, actually crossed the Atlantic by ship, after the two attempts of the Martinsyde crew proved abortive

26 Cover of a letter addressed by Captain (later Sir) John Alcock to his sister, Mrs Elsie Moseley, and flown by him in his converted Vickers Vimy bomber from Newfoundland to Ireland, 1919

so (actual flying time 25 hours). The crew of this aircraft, the NC-4, were given a great welcome when they arrived in Britain and were subsequently decorated by King George V. This flight, while marking the first aerial crossing of the Atlantic, lacks the interest of the *Daily Mail* attempts and, moreover, was not marked by any philatelic mementoes, since no mail was carried by the US flying boats.

During April 1919 the Sopwith team prepared for their flight. A week before the first trial flight was made, Dr J. Alex. Robinson, the Postmaster-General of Newfoundland, wrote to Captain Fenn, manager of the Sopwith team and enquired:

> On what terms will you carry a small official mail, the number of letters not to exceed ten, and the weight not to exceed one pound?
>
> As an alternative proposition, and subject to such limitations as may be agreed upon, on what terms will you carry a general letter mail?
>
> The above enquiries are made on the supposition that yours will be the first attempt to cross the Atlantic by airship.

Captain Fenn replied on 8 April and asked that the aircraft be allowed to carry 100 letters in addition to the official ten, and proposed a payment of $1 for this service. The Fenn-Robinson correspondence, together with the Postmaster-General's cheque for one dollar, are now preserved, along with other interesting relics of the flight, in the Fitzgerald Collection at the British Museum.

Dr Robinson accepted these conditions and the overprinting of a quantity of the 3c Caribou stamp was put in hand. A trial overprint (of which 15 copies are known) was made in a setting 22mm wide, but the setting actually adopted for the issued overprints measured only 19mm. Some 200 Caribous were overprinted at the office of the *Daily News* in St John's. Of these, 95 were used to frank the mail, 18 defective copies were destroyed, 11 were presented to officials and others, and the remaining 76 mint copies were sold at $25 each on behalf of the Marine Disasters Fund. Dr Robinson initialled the stamps on the reverse JAR but in 1933 a specimen was discovered by Cyril Harmer in the collection of an American, bearing the initials WC on the back. These proved to be the initials of William Campbell, Secretary of the Newfoundland GPO. The stamp eventually passed into the hands of Mrs Fitzgerald, whose collection was donated to the British Museum in 1951. Rumour has it that Mr Campbell initialled *four* stamps, but the British Museum specimen is certainly the only known unused copy. The Hawker airmail stamp is exceedingly rare in multiple form, there being only three mint pairs and a mint vertical strip of three in existence. The latter was for many years one of the gems in the Lichtenstein Collection, but it is now in the British Museum.

Hawker and Mackenzie-Grieve took off from Mount Pearl, near St John's, at 6.48 p.m. (BST) on 18 April. Bad weather, plus a defective cooling system in the engine, doomed the Sopwith flight to failure. Hawker was forced to ditch the aircraft at 9.30 a.m. the following morning, within sight of the Danish tramp steamer *Mary*, which rescued the airmen. The aircraft itself, together with its precious cargo, was salvaged four days later by the American ship *Lake Charlotteville*. The mailbag had suffered immersion in the sea and consequently the Hawker covers usually bear some sign of saltwater staining. One of the covers in the British Museum is actually minus its stamp, which was washed off by the sea-water. Its presence was proved, however, by the initials JAR in reverse, which had become imprinted where the stamp should have been. Conversely, the master of the *Lake Charlotteville*, Captain Wilvers, found three unused Hawkers in the mailbag and one of these, minus its gum, is now in the British Museum.

The second attempt on the Atlantic was made by the Martinsyde team barely an hour after the Sopwith plane took off. Unfortunately the *Raymor* crashed on take-off and both airmen were slightly injured. Major Morgan was advised not to make another attempt on health grounds and a month later his substitute, Lieut Biddlescombe, arrived. By this time the Vickers team had made their successful flight but the Martinsyde crew, determined to beat the Vickers flying time, made a second attempt on 17 July—again crashing on take-off. This ended the abortive Martinsyde flights, but the ill-fated *Raymor* has left her mark on aerophilately nonetheless.

On account of the short time-factor, type-set overprints could not be procured for the first Martinsyde flight. A small number of Caribous was, however, overprinted in manuscript AERIAL ATLANTIC MAIL in three lines (in the handwriting of Mr Campbell) and endorsed with the initials of Dr Robinson at the foot. It is thought that barely two dozen stamps were thus treated and fewer than a score have actually been recorded. The stamp was not sold over the post office counter, but was affixed to mail handed in for the flight; thus unused copies were never available. Yet two unused copies are in existence, both in the Fitzgerald Collection; both are attached to pieces of paper and both have an interesting story behind them. The first was originally on a cover handed in for franking by Major Raynham. He decided to add a postscript to his letter and after it had been franked he asked for it back. Somewhat absentmindedly he popped the letter into his coat pocket and forgot all about it. When he sold it, many years later, he apologised to the purchaser for the fact that it had not been postmarked.

The other unused Martinsyde was discovered in a desk at the GPO attached to a portion of an envelope. The capital As differ from those on the issued overprints so it may be regarded as an essay; it is believed that the capitals were changed to the more compressed form for reasons of space.

The Martinsyde manuscript Caribous were cancelled at St John's on 19 April. One cover has been recorded bearing the Hawker and Martinsyde Caribous side by side. This remarkable item was despatched by a newspaperman, Edwin Cleary, who opened a previously sealed envelope in order to incorporate more up-to-date news for the *Daily Express*. This unique cover, combining two of the greatest rarities of aerophilately, is one of the gems of the Fitzgerald Collection.

Mr Cleary was also responsible for the controversial Martinsyde type-set overprints, prepared in connection with the second attempt by Major Raynham. Caribou stamps in denominations of 1, 2, 3, 4, 5, 24 and 36c, together with examples of the 2c postcard and 3c envelope, were overprinted privately in five lines: 1ST ATLANTIC/AIR POST,/MARTINSYDE,/RAYNHAM,/MORGAN. The covers and cards (some 15 in all) were cancelled with the St John's registered rubber stamp on 17 May. The use of the registered handstamp was decidedly irregular and seems to indicate complaisance on the part of some postal official. Cleary was also responsible for several covers bearing unoverprinted Caribous, endorsed across the face: FIRST AIR POST X THE ATLANTIC. His motive in so doing was probably quite innocent; in view of the small quantity of stamps and covers he could never have produced them for financial gain. Being on the spot he was no doubt motivated by a desire to provide a philatelic memento of the Martinsyde flight. These stamps have been roundly condemned as bogus.

The sad story of the Martinsyde mail was rounded off farcically. On his return to England by sea Major Raynham, to whom the mailbag had been entrusted, forgot all about it until reminded of it by an official enquiry at the beginning of January 1920. The mail was surrendered to the authorities on 7 January and backstamped in London on that date—almost eight months after the date of cancellation at St John's.

Both Hawker and Raynham had made their attempts and failed before the next contestants arrived in Newfoundland. On 24 May Alcock and Brown with their Vickers *Vimy* disembarked at St John's from the ss *Glendevon* and their first trial flights were not made till a fortnight later. The Handley Page team, with their converted V/1500 bomber, had already taken up residence at Harbour Grace, but they took too long in getting their machine ready and the Vickers team had completed their successful Atlantic flight before the V/1500 was tuned up.

Dr Robinson, noting the simultaneous preparations of the Handley Page and Vickers teams, decided to entrust a small mail to both aircraft. For this purpose it was decided to charge $1 fee for each letter carried and the prepayment of this postage was to be denoted by special airmail stamps consisting of the 15c Cabot stamp of 1897 overprinted TRANS-ATLANTIC AIR POST 1919 ONE DOLLAR in four lines. Half the fee was credited to the Marine Disasters Fund, so this airmail stamp is also in the nature of a charity issue. Some of these stamps were used to frank the supplementary mail carried by the Martinsyde plane; thus it will be found on mail carried by *three* of the 1919 competitors. The Fitzgerald Collection contains a Martinsyde cover bearing this stamp.

A total of 9,970 stamps was produced on this occasion, which accounts for the comparatively low value set on this stamp. Even so, Alcock and Brown carried only 197 items franked with this stamp and it would seem that genuine flown Alcock covers are long overdue for a marked rise in price. At present this seems to be about £70-£150, depending on condition and interest. The Fitzgerald Collection contains a number of the Alcock covers, including the letters, and among these is an interesting item written by Sir John Alcock himself to his sister:

My Dear Elsie,

Just a hurried line before we start. This letter will travel with me in the official mail bag, the first mail to be carried over the Atlantic. Love to all,

Your loving brother,

Jack.

On 14 June the Vickers *Vimy* rose clumsily into the air, narrowly missing the houses and trees surrounding the airfield, and set a course for the open Atlantic. The aviators were hampered by unfavourable weather (fog below and dense cloud above) and to make matters worse their radio packed up shortly after take-off. Severe storms buffeted the frail craft as it droned steadily onward. Ice continually froze up the controls. At one point Alcock found the plane spinning towards the Atlantic; he barely managed to kick the rudder bar over and yank back the control column before the plane hit the waves. Some time after dawn the Irish coast loomed up and at 9.30 a.m. (BST) the *Vimy* crossed the coast of Galway. Near Clifden Alcock brought his machine down on what appeared to be a suitable patch of level grass, but this proved on contact to be a bog. The bomber sank into the soft turf and tipped forward on its nose, but the airmen scrambled out unhurt. They had successfully crossed the Atlantic in the time of 16 hours and 12 minutes.

Alcock and Whitten-Brown were given a tremendous reception on their triumphal journey to London. On 21 June they were received by King George V at Buckingham Palace and given the accolade of KBE. Typical of the men was their generous action in handing over £2,000 of their prize money to be shared out among the employees of Vickers and Rolls Royce who had built their machine. The Fitzgerald Collection contains a telegram sent by Alcock and Brown to the Vickers mechanics at St John's: 'Your hard work and splendid efforts have been amply rewarded. We did not let you down.' This telegram was sent by Marconi's radio station at Clifden shortly after the airmen landed.

Sir John Alcock was not destined to live long to enjoy his success. On 15 December of the same year he was killed in an air crash at Cote d'Evrard, on a flight to Paris. A sad memento of Alcock in the British Museum collection is his last pilot's licence, valid from August 1919 till February 1920.

The Handley Page team, pipped at the post, was determined

to fly the Atlantic by the southern route (via the Azores) to try and cut the time taken by Alcock and Brown. On 4 July the plane left Harbour Grace for Nova Scotia, but trouble in the oil system forced the pilot to make a crash landing at Parrsboro at 3.50 a.m. on the following day. The machine was badly damaged and this put an end to the Handley Page attempt. The mail carried by this plane, amounting to some 115 pieces, bore a special Handley Page oval rubber cachet on the reverse. The mail was forwarded to New York for connection with the airship R34 but arrived too late and was sent on to Europe by the *Mauretania* instead.

England to Australia

Undoubtedly the publicity given to the *Daily Mail* offer encouraged the Australian government to do likewise. On 19 March 1919 the Acting Prime Minister of Australia announced a prize of £10,000 for the first Australian aircrew to fly from England to Australia. The flight had to be completed in 720 hours before 31 December 1920. Even before March 1919, however, Australian airmen were laying plans for a flight to their home country, one of these being Captain Ross MacPherson Smith who subsequently won the race.

Five crews entered the contest. Of these, one crashed shortly after take-off killing both pilot and navigator and two others crashed at Corfu (one with fatal results for its crew). The other two made the trip to Australia successfully, but that made by Lieut Ray Parer and Lieut J. C. MacIntosh was not attempted till after the successful Smith flight had been accomplished.

The winning entry was a sister ship of the Atlantic Vickers *Vimy*, but flown this time by a crew of four: Captain Ross Smith (pilot), Lieut Keith Smith, his younger brother (navigator) and the two mechanics, Sergeants James Bennett and Wally Shiers. All four served in Number One Squadron, Australian Flying Corps. They took off from Weybridge airfield on Armistice Day 1919 and eventually reached Darwin in northern Australia on 10 December. Although they had won the prize, the airmen had a further 3,000 miles to fly in order to bring the plane to its official destination in Melbourne and the cross-continental flight, as hazardous as anything encountered previously, took twice as long to accomplish. Melbourne was not reached until 25 February.

A quantity of mail was carried on the Ross Smith flight and various letters added to the mail at different stages, so that the philatelic aspects of the flight are extremely complicated. Covers were endorsed with a three-line cachet PER VICKERS 'VIMY' AEROPLANE TO AUSTRALIA. During the trans-Australian stage of the flight the question of a special stamp for mail carried by the Smiths was mooted and eventually a large vignette in dark blue was produced and applied to the flown covers. It depicted maps of Britain and Australia with the inscriptions FIRST AERIAL POST and ENGLAND-AUSTRALIA. The dates of the flight also appeared so that this label prepared after the event is in the nature of a commemorative item. The Vickers *Vimy* bomber is depicted above the maps. The stamps were affixed to the covers and cancelled with an oval double-lined postmark. Approximately 130 covers were flown. The covers were forwarded to the addresses under plain wrapper, as a precaution against the theft of the souvenir vignette. Today these souvenirs of the England-Australia flight are very expensive, but an interesting modern counterpart, which is still freely available, is the material which was produced in November-December 1969 in connection with the 50th anniversary of this flight. In November 1969 a Comet XR 399, commanded by Squadron Leader J. L. Buist, flew from RAF Lyneham in England to Darwin, Australia in 3 days 19 hours 32 minutes (actual flying time 24 hours 10 minutes). Souvenir mail flown on this occasion was franked with the British stamp commemorating the 1919 flight, with a special pictorial hand-stamp showing the Vickers *Vimy* on a map of Australia. The flown covers were cacheted at the various staging points en route and postmarked on arrival in Darwin on 16 November. The time taken on this flight compared well with the original 136 hours 55 minutes flying time of the Smith brothers.

The following month a London-Sydney air race was organised by the Royal Aero Club of the United Kingdom and the Royal Federation of Aero Clubs of Australia under the auspices of the BP oil company. Mail flown on that occasion was also franked with the special 1s 9d airmail stamp showing the Vickers *Vimy* and a map of the route, with a relatively plain circular postmark inscribed LONDON-SYDNEY AIR RACE dated 17 December. The mail on this occasion was backstamped at the various scheduled stopping places: La Baule, Athens, Karachi, Calcutta, Singapore and Darwin.

These commercially inspired covers at least offer the opportunity to the collector of acquiring at reasonable cost a souvenir connected in some way with the original event, in cases where the original flight was either undocumented by flown covers or the flown covers and cards are now excessively rare. Among the other recent anniversaries in aviation commemorated by flights producing special covers were the diamond jubilee of Blériot's cross-Channel flight of 1909 and the 50th anniversary of the first international airmail from the United Kingdom, from Hounslow to Le Bourget in November 1919.

First South Atlantic Flight 1922

While the Anglo-Saxon races had dominated the early trans-Atlantic flights by the northern route, it was left to the Latin races to pioneer the routes across the South Atlantic. On 30 March 1922 two officers of the Portuguese navy, Captain Sacedura Cabral and Captain Coutinho, took off from Lisbon in a seaplane. They reached Las Palmas in the Canary Isles on the same day but were then delayed for two days by bad weather. Successive hops took them to the Bay of Gonda and then to St Vincent in the Cape Verde Islands on 4 April. Bad weather again delayed them and it was not until 17 April that they were able to embark on the most dangerous part of the flight, across the open Atlantic. After a flight of 1,800 kilometres engine trouble forced them down in the ocean near the rock of St Paul more than 300 miles east of the Brazilian coast. The Portuguese government despatched a second aircraft by ship but this crashed on a trial flight from St Paul. A third aeroplane, however, was procured and in this machine Cabral and Coutinho made the flight to Pernambuco and thence to Rio. Despite the bad luck which marred this flight it stands out as a success from the navigational point of view. Coutinho's navigation was so precise that at no time did the aviators doubt their exact location. When they were forced down at St Paul, an error of a degree either way in navigation would have been disastrous. From the aerophilatelic viewpoint, however, this flight is extremely disappointing. No mail was flown on this occasion so that no souvenirs of the actual flight exist. The following year Portugal made amends by releasing a series of 16 stamps commemorating the flight. The stamps were on sale for a few hours only and were the subject of tremendous speculation, although

27 Airmail Rarities *1–3* Newfoundland air stamps of 1919 for the Hawker, Alcock and Martinsyde flights *4* Austria, 1920. Unissued 2k airmail stamp *5* Finland 1930 Zeppelin overprints, one showing the error ' 1830 ' in the date *6* Bulgaria, 1927-8. 1 on 6 leva with surcharge inverted *7* Switzerland 1938 Aviation Fund. These stamps were not sold to the public in mint condition; this example is possibly unique

28 Postcard from Lord Willingdon, Viceroy of India, despatched from the British Residency, Cairo to Bombay on the first through aerial mail between Great Britain and India, January 1919. Note the commemorative cachet and Karachi censor mark

29 Cover bearing the official vignette of the England–Australia First Aerial Post and the oval postmark used on mail carried by Ross and Keith Smith, 1919–20

nowadays they are reasonably cheap. They bore portraits of the pilot and navigator and showed the seaplane and a fifteenth-century galleon, symbolising the ancient and modern methods by which the Portuguese had come to South America.

The Rome-Tokyo Flights

The Italian poet and playwright, Gabriele D'Annunzio, made a name for himself as an aviator by his daring raids on Trieste and Vienna during the First World War but although he never again participated actively in aviation his influence in its post-war development in Italy was considerable. One of his ambitions had been to stage a mass flight of aeroplanes from Italy to the far ends of the globe. These ambitions were subsequently realised, but D'Annunzio had to leave their realisation to other men. He was particularly interested in a flight by a squadron of Italian aircraft to the Far East and in connection with this project he drew up plans with his wartime colleagues. In the end, however, he was too preoccupied with his swashbuckling adventures in Fiume and Dalmatia to take part.

The start was to have been made on 15 October 1919, but the flight was continually delayed in the hope that D'Annunzio would be able to leave Fiume (which his irregular troops were holding for Italy in defiance of the Yugoslav and Allied authorities). By February 1920, however, the flight could be delayed no longer and the squadron of 11 Ansalmo 300 h.p. aircraft had to take off without him. The mass flight began from Rome on 13 February and went in 27 stages, via Salonika, Smyrna, Adalia, Baghdad, Bandar Abbas, Karachi, Delhi, Hemed, Shanghai, Peking and Osaka to Tokyo. Two pilots were killed en route in plane crashes, while five planes dropped out in the Balkan hop between Valona and Salonika. Ultimately only the planes piloted by Ferrarin and Masiero reached their destination safely on 31 May, having covered a distance of over 14,000 kilometres. Philatelically there was little to show for this flight. At Charbar, which Ferrarin and Masiero reached on 4 March, the former took aboard three postcards addressed by the sender, a Mr E. Edwards, to the Director of Persian Gulf Telegraphs at Karachi, with the hope 'that he was not violating any official formalities'. These cards, autographed by Ferrarin, are now among the great rarities of the period.

In 1925 the Italian navigator, the Marchese de Pinedo, made

the greatest flight attempted up to that time. Altogether he covered some 43,000 miles in his round the world flight, without escort and with the minimum of assistance. On 20 April 1925 De Pinedo and his mechanic left Ostia near Rome and flew in a Savoia S-55 hydroplane to India, arriving at Karachi on 5 May. The flight was delayed by three days while repairs were effected to the right float of the seaplane which had been damaged by heavy seas near Charbar. From there they flew on via Bombay and Calcutta where some mail was picked up. This consisted of 124 letters and 32 postcards for delivery in Rangoon, Burma, and some 93 letters for onward transmission to Australia. This mail received a violet rectangular cachet showing a map of India and a rough outline of the Savoia seaplane, with the caption ITALIAN WORLD AIR FLIGHT INDIA 1926. Initially De Pinedo was asked to autograph the covers and this he proceeded to do, but when the promoters of this private airmail refused to donate 20 rupees per letter to Italian charities, he promptly cut off the portions of each cover bearing his signature. The mutilated covers were duly delivered to the Italian Consulate at Melbourne and returned to the senders, but at no stage did they actually pass through the government postal service. Their status is therefore the somewhat curious one of flown souvenirs without official validity.

De Pinedo reached the Philippine Islands on 20 August 1925 and there he was entrusted with quantities of airmail which had the sanction of the authorities. Various cachets showing a biplane inscribed VIA PINEDO'S FLIGHT ROUND THE WORLD were applied to this mail, with the names of the various pick-up points inscribed on the lower wings of the biplane and the date placed on either side of the fuselage. This airmail extended over the entire range of the archipelago, from Zamboanga in the south (where De Pinedo first landed in the Philippines) to Aparri in the extreme north. Covers flown from Zamboanga, Cebu, Antimonau and Corregidor to Manila are known but in some cases only a handful were carried.

On 16 September De Pinedo left Aparri on his flight to Japan. The postage stamps on flown covers were cancelled with a special postmark in the shape of an aeroplane, while a cachet inscribed COMM F DE PINEDO'S AIRPLANE SAVOIA 1925 ROME-PHILIPPINES-TOKYO was applied to the front of the covers while the biplane cachet, similar to those previously used but inscribed APARRI on the lower plane, was struck on the reverse flap. Some

474 covers were flown by De Pinedo from the Philippines to Japan.

From the Philippines De Pinedo flew to Shangai in September and then flew to Tokyo on 21 September carrying a mailbag containing 50 letter cacheted FIRST AIR MAIL CHINA-JAPAN. On the return flight from Tokyo to Shanghai in October 1925 De Pinedo was to have picked up a mailbag containing 80 letters for Hong Kong and 29 addressed to Rome. This mail, posted in Nanking, should have travelled by express train all night in order to reach the pilot before his start the following morning. Unfortunately one of the periodic revolutions, to which China was then prone, broke out that night and sporadic fighting between Government forces and mutinous troops flared up. The revolutionary soldiers dynamited parts of the Nanking-Shanghai railway line and thus delayed the train which did not reach Shanghai until the day after De Pinedo's departure and therefore had to travel to their destinations by land and sea. These covers bore a four-line cachet inscribed FIRST AERIAL MAIL—SHANGHAI-HONG KONG—CARRIED BY MAJOR DE PINEDO.

Madrid-Manila 1926

Another of the great flights of the 1920s was that carried out by Spanish military aviators who left Madrid on 5 April 1926 and reached Manila in the Philippines on 13 May. The aircraft was crewed by Captains Gallarza and Loriga and they carried a small mail consisting of 16 letters. These covers bore various cachets PRIMER CORREO AEREO MADRID-MANILA or POR AVION MADRID MANILA. On their arrival two large cachets were applied to the backs of the envelopes, one showing a biplane not unlike those used for the De Pinedo airmail but inscribed MADRID TO MANILA FLIGHTS ACCOMPANIED BY SPANISH AVIATORS MANILA PHILIPPINE ISLANDS. The other also showed an aeroplane but in a different type, with the coats of arms of the Philippines, the United States and Spain and the inscription RAID MADRID-MANILA. Subsequently both Spain and the Philippines issued stamps to celebrate this flight. The Spanish series consisted of Red Cross charity stamps. Stamps in denominations of 15c, 20c, 30c, 40c and 4 pesetas featured the Bréguet-19 aircraft used by Gallarza and Loriga with a map of their route along the coast of north Africa across Palestine and India to South East Asia and the Philippines. These stamps were not designed for airmail use and unsold remainders were subsequently overprinted to mark the 25th anniversary of the coronation of King Alfonso XIII. The Philippines overprinted the contemporary definitive series with inscriptions AIR MAIL 1926 MADRID-MANILA and a propeller emblem in the centre. Two printings were made of this overprint and in the second printing one stamp in every sheet of 100 appeared with the left blade of the propeller omitted.

Newfoundland-Rome 1927

In May 1927 Commander De Pinedo made an attempt on the trans-Atlantic route, flying from Trepassey, Newfoundland, to Rome. The Newfoundland postal authorities were always alert to the possibilities of despatching mail by air and lost no time in arranging an airmail on this occasion. For this purpose it was decided to permit a limited amount of letter mail, not exceeding one ounce per letter, to be transmitted and the airmail rate was fixed at 60c. To this end a small quantity of the 60c stamp of the 1897 commemorative series (portraying King Henry VII) was overprinted in red AIR MAIL DE PINEDO 1927 in three lines. Some 258 of these stamps, out of a total printing of three sheets (300), were sold over the post office counter, 20 were presented to De Pinedo, 18 presented to various officials and 4 destroyed on account of damage. Of those sold some 225 were used to frank letters. In addition about 75 other covers were flown but franked with ordinary unoverprinted Henry VII 60c stamps. Although the so-called 'supplementary mail' was smaller these covers are not rated so highly as those bearing the special stamp. Very few De Pinedo stamps were preserved in unused condition and as a result they are now priced at thousands of pounds. The use of the stamp of 1897 was a delicate compliment to De Pinedo since it had formed part of a set originally issued to commemorate the quatercentenary of Henry VII's commission to the Italian navigator, John Cabot, to head an expedition in quest of the 'new found land' on the other side of the Atlantic.

De Pinedo took off from Trepassey in his aircraft *Santa Maria II* on 23 May 1927 but was forced to land on the ocean about 200 miles from the Azores and had to be towed into Horta bay. From there he flew in easy stages to Rome which he reached on 16 June. The mailbag was not handed over to the post office till 22 June, but the clerks began backstamping the covers with the date 16 June until it was decided that they should bear the date of actual delivery to the post office. Covers have therefore been recorded with the Rome arrival postmark of 16 June, 22 June or both dates side by side. This is perhaps De Pinedo's best known flight, mainly because of the fame imparted by the rare airmail stamp which has made his name a household word to philatelists. Six year later, on 2 September 1933, the Marchese De Pinedo met his death when his aircraft crashed on take-off at Floyd Bennett Field, Brooklyn, New York, at the commencement of a solo flight to Baghdad.

New York-Paris 1927

Perhaps no flight has so stirred the imagination as that made by Charles Lindbergh from New York to Paris in May 1927. Although some eight years had elapsed since the first flights across the Atlantic Lindbergh's achievement was sensational. For the first time a solo flight of the Atlantic had been success-fully attempted and the feat was all the more remarkable since Lindbergh flew non-stop from the United States, over New-foundland and Ireland to France, a distance of 3,600 miles in 33 hours 31 minutes.

As early as 1919 a wealthy hotel owner, Raymond Orteig, offered $25,000 for the first non-stop flight between New York and Paris. Although the Atlantic was bridged that summer no aeroplane existed at the time which was capable of a sustained flight of that duration without stopping to refuel, nor, indeed, could the aero engines of the period be relied upon to con-tinue for such a long time without seizing up. By 1926, how-ever, several pilots had decided to attempt the non-stop crossing. In September of that year the French aviator, Rene Fonck, took off from Roosevelt Field, Long Island in a Sikorsky with a crew of three. This aeroplane crashed on take-off and two of the crew were killed. The following April two American naval officers were killed in Virginia while testing their machine prior to an attempt on the New York-Paris flight. In May 1927 two French airmen, Charles Nungesser and Francois Coli, took off from Paris in their plane *Oiseau Blanc* (White Bird) attempting the more difficult crossing from east to west. Somewhere over the Atlantic Nungesser and Coli met with tragedy for neither they nor their plane were ever seen again.

In the same month Clarence Chamberlain and Bert Acosta, set up a new record for endurance, keeping their Bellanca aeroplane aloft for 51 hours. Barely a week later, however, on 20 May 1927, Charles Lindbergh left Roosevelt Field in his Ryan monoplane, *Spirit of St Louis*, carrying 2,750 pounds of fuel and very little else—no radio, no sextant and no parachute! He took off at 7.52 a.m. and flew northwards, crossing Nova Scotia and Newfoundland. The flight was hampered by fog but otherwise the weather was favourable. Sleep was the main enemy, but after the Irish coast was sighted Lindbergh was too excited to doze off any longer and flew on steadily to Le Bourget where he landed in the evening of 21 May. His aircraft still held 85 gallons of fuel when he touched down. Two weeks later Clarence Chamberlain and Charles Levine were to fly non-stop from New York to Germany but in the popular annals of aviation they are all but forgotten, so overshadowed was their achievement by the Lindbergh flight.

As with so many other of the great pioneer flights of this period no mail or souvenirs were produced for the aerophilatelists of later generations to compete for. Subsequently Lindbergh went on a series of goodwill flights to Latin America and not only were covers flown on these occasions but several of the countries which he visited produced commemorative stamps in his honour. The greatest honour, however, came from the United States which took the unprecedented step of issuing a stamp on 18 June 1927 showing the *Spirit of St Louis* spanning the Atlantic with the route of the flight indicated. The stamp bore the inscription LINDBERGH AIRMAIL, the first, and, so far the only, occasion on which an American stamp has borne the name of a living American. In September of the same year France issued two stamps to honour the visit of the American Legion to France, marking the 10th anniversary of the entry of the United States into the First World War and the common design of these stamps featured the Ryan monoplane over the Atlantic, flanked by profiles of Lafayette and George Washington. In October 1930 Spain issued a series of air stamps in connection with the Spanish-American Exhibition. The 1 peseta value portrayed Lindbergh and showed his aeroplane. In the bottom right-hand corner appeared the tiny black cat which Lindbergh carried as a mascot on his flight.

London-London 1927

The New York to Paris flight sponsored by Raymond Orteig had its more northerly counterpart in a flight from London (Ontario) to London (England) sponsored by Charles Burns, president of the Carling Breweries of Canada, who offered a prize of $25,000 for the first successful crossing. Some 80 Canadian pilots applied for this venture and from them Captain Tulley was eventually selected to make the attempt. The promoters secured the approval of the Canadian postal department to carry a small airmail and for this purpose special 25 cent stamps were lithographed by Lawson & Jones of London Ontario in green and yellow on white paper. Only 100 stamps were printed and of these 97 were affixed to letters. The design of this stamp showed the top of the globe and an aeroplane, with portraits of Sir John Carling, founder of Carling Breweries, and Captain Tulley in oval frames on either side. There is an old superstition among aviators that they must not be photographed before a flight. Perhaps something of this superstition also applied to appearing on stamps before a flight since, with the exception of the Figueroa stamp of Chile (see Chapter 7), no pilot has been portrayed on stamps issued before an important flight.

Tulley took off from London Ontario and flew via Harbour Grace in Newfoundland. Somewhere beyond Newfoundland the aircraft is thought to have run into thick fog and crashed into the Atlantic without trace. Neither the aeroplane, the pilot nor the mailbag were ever found and therefore this flight is remembered solely by the three remaining examples of the stamp in unused condition. Two of these are now in the Fitzgerald Collection in the British Museum and the third is currently priced at $6,500 in the Sanabria *World Airmail Catalogue*—surely one of the most underpriced rarities of philately. The fact that this stamp is relatively undervalued is due to comparative ignorance of the flight. Few collectors know of its existence and it has never gained the publicity accorded to the other trans-Atlantic flights, no doubt on account of the fact that it was unsuccessful. Shortly after this tragic flight rather crude reproductions of the London to London stamp were produced as 'space fillers' but since the fabricator of these imitations had never seen an original they differ considerably in design and colour.

French Catapult Mail 1928

In the 1920s the most famous of the French trans-Atlantic liners was the giant *Ile de France* which plied regularly on the run from Le Havre to New York. As part of her cargo this liner carried the mails between the two countries and letters usually took six or seven days on the journey. In a bid to speed up this service for the more important letters an experiment was carried out in August 1928. The liner carried a seaplane which could be catapulted from the deck and into the air when the liner was still a day's sailing from the port of Le Havre. By this means it was possible to despatch a quantity of letter mail and expedite its handling. On 8 August and again on 12 August this experiment was carried out with satisfactory results. No special markings were applied to the covers flown in this way, although they can usually be identified easily from the postmarks. On the next run of the *Ile de France*, however, it was decided to produce special stamps to prepay the 10 francs airmail fee. The production of these stamps was authorised by the French Consul-General in New York and the work of surcharging the 90c (Berthelot) and 1.50f (Pasteur) stamps was entrusted to the French Printing and Publishing Company of New York. These stamps are known with the surcharge inverted and with varying spaces in the setting of the inscription. A total of 3,000 of the 90c and 1,000 of the 1.50f stamps were thus surcharged. A six-line cachet was applied to covers flown by seaplane from the *Ile de France* on 23 August inscribed AOUT-SEPTEMBRE 1928 —PREMIER LIAISON POSTALE AERIENNE—TRANSATLANTIQUE—PAR HYDRAVION LANCE PAR CATAPULTE—DE L'ILE-DE-FRANCE—PILOTE LIEUTENANT DE VAISSEAU L DEMOURGET. These covers were postmarked on arrival at Le Havre with the octagonal cancellation inscribed NEW YORK-LE HAVRE, normally employed on ship's mail. Although this experiment was highly successful it was felt that the time saved was not sufficient to justify the expense of the service and as a result it was never repeated. The 10f surcharges and the 'catapult mail' covers are now among the most expensive items of French aerophilately.

Although the French discontinued the catapult mail service it was taken up enthusiastically the following year by the Germans. The first mail by catapult plane left the liner *Bremen* on 22 July 1929 when the ship was a day's voyage from New York. On 2 August mail was flown from the ship to the port of Bremen in the same manner. Special cachets were used on the covers carried on both occasions but no special stamps were provided. Subsequently the *Bremen* despatched mail by catapult plane on numerous occasions to New York, Amsterdam, Cherbourg and Southampton and to Bremen for onward transmission to Berlin or Cologne. This service was extended in 1930 to the liner *Europa* and in 1930-1 mail was also flown from land to the liners *Bremen*, *Europa* and *Columbus* from Cologne via Cherbourg. In every case distinctive cachets were applied to flown covers and quite a substantial collection can be made of the German catapult mails in themselves. The service came to an end in the winter of 1931 but was temporarily resumed in the summer of 1932 but ceased to operate in July of that year, the last flight being from the *Europa* to Southampton on 5 July.

Kingsford Smith Flights

It seems incredible that four decades ago the Pacific Ocean had never been crossed by air. In 1919 several attempts, some abortive, some successful, had been made to fly the Atlantic and in 1927 Colonel Charles Lindbergh was the first man to fly across the ocean non-stop, but up to that time the Pacific remained an unanswerable challenge to the aviators of the world. Two Australian veterans of the Royal Flying Corps, however, had long dreamt of flying from America to Australia but working independently lacked the means to turn their dreams into reality.

C. E. Kingsford Smith and C. T. P. Ulm did not meet each other until early in 1927 when they were both employed by Interstate Flying Services, an airline operating from Sydney, New South Wales. Together they planned to fly the Pacific but wisely decided that a flight round Australia first would give them much-needed experience of long-distance flying, as well as providing some useful publicity and perhaps financial backing for the more ambitious flight.

Previously Captain E. J. Jones, of the Australian Department of Civil Aviation, had flown round the continent in 22 days 11 hours. Smith and Ulm were determined to complete the 7,500 mile circuit in half the time. Using a seven-year-old Bristol Tourer, they took off from Sydney on 19 June 1927 and flying via Camooweal (Queensland), Darwin, Broome (Western Australia), Perth and Melbourne they returned to

Sydney on 29 June, having established a record flight of 750 miles on one stage of the journey. The resultant publicity had the desired effect and the Prime Minister of New South Wales announced that his government were prepared to provide £3,500 towards the cost of a trans-Pacific flight.

Smith and Ulm sailed to San Francisco on the ss *Tahiti* and arrived in the United States in August 1927, to begin the planning and preparations for the long flight back. The ensuing months were punctuated by numerous setbacks as the aviators attempted to raise the necessary money. On the one hand they secured admirable co-operation from the United States Navy and the British Ambassador, as well as gifts and loans from Australian businessmen and money raised in Sydney by the Returned Soldiers' and Sailors' Imperial League, but the biggest bombshell came when the New South Wales elections of 1927 brought to power a new government which promptly cancelled the guarantee of its predecessor. The disastrous outcome of the Dole Race, an attempt to fly from San Francisco to Honolulu, made the Smith-Ulm project seem extremely foolhardy and the New South Wales premier strongly urged the fliers to abandon their project.

By this time they had bought a tri-motor Fokker, which they were now forced to sell to pay off their creditors. At the last minute an American millionaire, Captain G. Allan Hancock, came to the rescue, purchased the plane from them for $16,000 and agreed to let them fly it to Australia. Not only was Hancock's generosity unbounded during the remainder of their stay in America but, on the successful completion of the flight, he made them a gift of the aircraft.

Preparations for the flight began in earnest in April 1928. The plane chosen for the flight was a Fokker monoplane similar to that used on several long-distance record flights. It was powered by three Wright Whirlwind J5C engines, each developing 220 h.p. This relatively large aircraft enabled the crew for the flight to be increased to four. Two Americans, Harry Lyon and Jim Warner, were recruited as navigator and radio operator respectively. At 8.45 a.m. on 31 May 1928 the Fokker, named the *Southern Cross*, took off from Oakland Airport and, flying over the Golden Gate, headed out to sea. Twenty-six hours later they sighted the snow-capped bulk of Mauna Kea, the extinct volcano in eastern Hawaii. An hour later the distinctive shape of Diamond Head on Oahu came into view and at 12.17 p.m.

on 1 June they touched down at Wheeler Field near Honolulu, after a flight of 2,408 miles in 27 hours 25 minutes with 130 gallons of fuel still in reserve.

After a good night's sleep the aviators made the comparatively short hop to Barking Sands, on the island of Kauai. Shortly after 5 a.m. on 3 June a heavily laden *Southern Cross* rose into the air and headed on a southerly course for Fiji. Bad luck hit the airmen on the second major leg of the flight. First the radio broke down, then violent rainstorms and exceptionally bad visibility added to the hazards of the flight. The weather improved after they had crossed the Equator just before midnight and the sight of the Southern Cross constellation glimmering on the port bow was taken as a good omen.

More violent storms hit the plane as dawn approached on 4 June but still they battled on. Then, as the weather improved, they ran into the Trade Wind which threatened to blow them off course. The fuel tanks were beginning to get low when, shortly after 1 p.m., Fiji showed up as a small brown dome on the horizon. At 3.45 p.m., after a flight of 34 hours 23 minutes, the *Southern Cross* landed on the Albert Park Sports Oval.

This was the trickiest landing of the entire flight. The sportsground was a mere 400 yards in length and the Fijian authorities had tried to improve the approach by uprooting the telegraph poles and cutting down the trees in the vicinity. An awkward problem was the fact that the park was 12 feet below the level of the road and Kingsford Smith narrowly missed it as he brought the machine in over the field at 65 m.p.h. The wheels touched the turf halfway down the field and the pilot just managed to 'ground loop' the plane before hitting the tree-lined bank at the far end. The flight from Barking Sands to Suva was 3,138 miles in length. In terms of distance it had been surpassed by the Lindbergh flight from America to France (3,600 miles) the previous year, but in view of the far greater hazards of weather and navigation involved, the flight to Suva must be regarded as one of the great achievements in the early annals of flight.

The aviators received a tumultuous welcome in Fiji. A crowd of more than 10,000 people turned out to greet them on arrival and during the next two days they were feted and garlanded wherever they went. The main problem, however, was to find a runway long enough for them to take off again with a heavy fuel load. They spent the next day prospecting for a likely site. Smith toured the islands in the government vessel *Andi Beti* and found an admirable runway on the beach at Naselai. On Wednesday evening, 6 June, the crew of the *Southern Cross* attended a ball given in their honour and were presented with a tortoiseshell casket containing 200 sovereigns which had been collected by the people of Suva.

The following day the *Southern Cross* flew over to Naselai beach and fuelled in readiness for the flight to Brisbane. Petrol was brought ashore by islanders in surf-boats and the tedious business of filling the tanks took far longer than had been anticipated so that the take-off had to be delayed till the afternoon of 8 June. At 2.52 p.m. they lifted from the beach with 900 gallons of petrol, after a run of 1,000 yards. After four hours' flying the *Southern Cross* ran into the worst storm of the entire flight. Apart from the buffeting which the machine sustained, the intense cold began to affect the engine revs, and in order to keep the plane headed into the storm it was necessary to dive it at speeds up to 105 knots (its cruising speed was normally around 80). This dangerous operation lasted for five hours, but shortly before midnight the weather improved and the storm abated.

Hours of blind flying had thrown the plane off course and the Australian coast was crossed at Balline, 110 miles south of Brisbane. Just after 10 a.m. on 9 June they landed at Eagle Farm airfield. The crew of the *Southern Cross* were greeted by the Governor of Queensland, Sir John Goodwin, and the Premier, Mr McCormack, and a cheering crowd of several thousands. The hooters and klaxons of 5,000 motor cars provided a deafening reception as the aviators stepped down from their plane. They were swept away to a tremendous civic welcome in Brisbane, followed by a State Reception that evening. The last lap of the epic flight was the comparatively uneventful flight to Sydney the following morning. When they arrived shortly after 3 p.m. they were greeted by a crowd of more than 300,000 at the airfield, while the entire million and a quarter inhabitants of Sydney turned out to cheer them on their triumphant drive into the city. Subsequently they got a heroes' welcome in Melbourne, Perth and Canberra.

Later in the year the *Southern Cross* set up another record, by flying the Tasman Sea to New Zealand, and in 1931 came the great flights linking England and Australia. Charles Kingsford Smith's services to aviation earned him a knighthood, the honorary rank of Air Commodore and the distinction of philatelic commemoration in his own lifetime. Australia issued 2d, 3d and 6d stamps in March 1931 showing the *Southern Cross* spanning the hemispheres and bearing the inscription KINGSFORD SMITH'S WORLD FLIGHTS. Both Australia and New Zealand issued stamps in a common design in 1958 to commemorate the 30th anniversary of the trans-Tasman flight. The stamps portrayed Smith in flying helmet and goggles and depicted the *Southern Cross* and the constellation.

On 19 March 1931 Kingsford Smith inaugurated the airmail service between Melbourne and Sydney. Some 800 covers were flown, of which 320 were autographed by the pilot. This service terminated on 26 June of the same year on account of the economic depression of the country. In April 1931 Sir Charles Kingsford Smith flew from Port Darwin in the *Southern Cross* to Akyab. There mail was transferred to aircraft of Imperial Airways and flown via Calcutta, Delhi and Karachi to London. A rectangular cachet was applied to flown covers inscribed COMMONWEALTH OF AUSTRALIA—AUSTRALIA-ENGLAND—FIRST OFFICIAL AIR MAIL FLIGHT. FROM MELBOURNE, AUSTRALIA TO LONDON, ENGLAND. Approximately 9,000 covers were carried. In November of the same year Kingsford Smith flew from Australia to Alor Star in the Straits Settlements (Malaya) and rescued mail which had been stranded there after an aircraft had broken down. On 3 December he flew on from Malaya to England, arriving at Croydon on 16 December. A special violet cachet was applied to the mail inscribed SPECIAL AIR MAIL FLIGHT NOV 1931 AUSTRALIA-ENGLAND. About 50,000 items were carried on this occasion so covers from this flight are relatively plentiful.

In connection with Kingsford Smith's trans-Tasman flights of 1928 mail was also flown. With Flight Lieutenant Ulm he flew in the *Southern Cross* from Sydney on 10 September to Christchurch, New Zealand. On arrival on the 11th Ulm was sworn in as a temporary postal official, as demanded by New Zealand postal regulations, and then delivered the mailbag to the head postmaster of Christchurch. On each cover New Zealand stamps were affixed to cover the New Zealand portion of the postage and these were cancelled with the Christchurch postmark. Both Kingsford Smith and Ulm autographed the covers, of which only ten are believed to exist.

7

Internal Airmails

Although sporadic attempts at mail-carrying by aeroplane had been made during and before the First World War it was not until the cessation of hostilities that the peaceful applications of aircraft could be seriously exploited. At the beginning of 1919 all of the major belligerents (including those recently defeated) possessed large fleets of aircraft and vast numbers of trained aircrew and ground staff. While passenger aeroplanes were yet to be developed the aircraft in existence at the end of the war were ideally suited to the transportation of small freight such as newspapers and mail where speed in transmission could be an advantage.

Much of the glamour attached to flying in the twenties resulted from the spectacular flights by intrepid aviators but, as a rule, many years elapsed before the routes they pioneered could be used by commercial airlines. Instead the early aviation companies concentrated on the establishment of air routes within a country or a comparatively limited area. Nowadays most countries rely heavily on sophisticated networks of local airways for the carriage of letter mail and a surprisingly large volume of mail is now handled by air at some stage in its transmission. Twenty years ago, however, this was the exception rather than the rule, while, in the 1920s, the carriage of letters by aeroplane was still a sufficiently notable event as to require special postmarks, cachets and even stamps to denote the fact. The internal airmails of the world in that decade are consequently legion and diverse and it would require a series of volumes to do justice to this period alone. Space permits only a few generalisations concerning the development of internal airmails, but those countries which, because of geographic or economic factors, developed an internal airways system at an early stage, are discussed in greater detail.

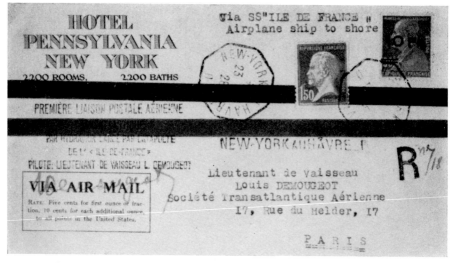

30 First Canal Zone—US airmail, October 1920. An explanatory cachet indicated that the flight had to be abandoned on account of 'impossible weather nearing Jamaica'. The mail was subsequently sent by steamship

31 Cover carried by catapult aircraft from the liner *Ile de France* to the American coast, 23 August 1928. The cover, bearing the cachet and signature of the pilot, Lieutenant Louis Demougeot, was addressed to himself

32-33 Canadian First Flight covers of the 1930s. Numerous different pictorial cachets were used on inaugural flights in Canada before the Second World War

In general, the countries which readily adopted aviation in the 1920s were those whose difficult terrain made surface communication by road, rail or river, hazardous if not impracticable, or whose vast area made surface communication a relatively tedious process. Thus among the pioneers of internal airways Canada, Colombia and the United States figure prominently. Other countries, though relatively small in area, had a high density of population coupled with a high degree of literacy and highly organised commerce, all of which combined to make airmail traffic a lucrative proposition. In this category came countries like Germany and Great Britain which led the way in the development of air services in Europe. Most countries of the civilised world made some attempt, with varying degrees of success, to establish civil airlines in the 1920s and almost every country could produce some examples of internal airmail. The decade from 1919 to 1929 witnessed the greatest developments in civil aviation and it was in this period that the basis for the internal networks of the present day was laid. This decade saw the greatest activity in aerophilately, with a phenomenal output of airmail stamps, both official and semi-official, special cachets and cancellations, and souvenir cards and covers. Consequently this period has been intensively studied and the literature on the subject is immense. Some of the more important catalogues, monographs and handbooks are listed in the select bibliography at the end of this book.

Canada

Canada in the 1920s was still a developing country and large areas of the north and west remained to be opened up. Communications in these remote areas were often non-existent, or consisted of relatively primitive lake and river transport. The aeroplane, whether fitted with wheels, floats or skis, was an ideal and adaptable medium for rapid communication over long distances and difficult country so it was hardly surprising that this method should be embraced so readily and to such a large extent. The mail flights of the 1920s and 1930s fell into two major categories, those by private companies who may or may not have held a contract from the Post Office, and those by the later, and larger airlines which had regular contracts from the Post Office for the carriage of mail over regular air routes.

In the first category the private companies were privileged

under Post Office sanction, to issue their own airmail stamps for use on letters and parcels carried by their aircraft. The Post Office exercised a very strict control over the issue of these stamps, so that they were never prone to the excesses which marred the semi-official issues of some other countries. As a result the great majority of the Canadian air stamps are scarce even in mint condition, while examples used on covers are often extremely rare.

Mention has already been made, in Chapter 5, of Canada's first air stamp, the 'Zeppelin' stamp of 1918 produced for the Toronto-Ottawa flight in August that year. In the ensuing decade there was a number of similar stamps, issued for a specific flight such as Toronto-New York (1919), Toronto-Hamilton (1924), the tragic London-London flight (1927) and Moose Jaw-Winnipeg (1928). Although of great interest and value these special issues are outside the scope of this chapter. The first of the commercial air lines to issue its own stamps was Laurentide Air Service Ltd which produced 25c denominations in green or red in 1924-5. These stamps were used on flights between Rouyn and various points such as Haileybury, Larder Lake and Three Rivers. It was on the inaugural flight from Rouyn to Three Rivers in January 1925 that the world's first aerial stowaway was detected. Northern Air Service, which also operated in the Haileybury-Rouyn district, issued 25c blue stamps in 1925 depicting a biplane in flight.

Jack V. Elliott formed an aviation company in 1926 under his name and issued 25c stamps with a letterpress design on a yellow background. The inaugural flight of this service took place on 6 March 1926 between Rolling Portage and Red Lake and return. Shortly afterwards the company was renamed the Elliott-Fairchild Air Service and similar stamps with a re-designed inscription were used on mail. In August of the same year the company changed its name to Elliott-Fairchild Air Transport Ltd and in October Elliott's name was dropped from the title. All of the latter issues of the company, with and without Elliott's name, featured a flying boat over a lake scene.

Patricia Airways and Exploration Co. issued 5, 10 and 25c stamps in 1926, the two lower denominations consisting of surcharges overprinted on the 25c value. The stamps were also overprinted with the names of the various places served— Haileybury and Rouyn, and Sioux Lookout and Red Lake or Red Lake alone. Numerous variations seem to have been deliberately perpetrated in this issue, with the use of different colours of ink for the overprints, or by inverting or doubling the overprint. Evidence suggests that these errors and varieties were deliberately fabricated for sale to collectors and for this reason the stamps of Patricia Airways, alone of the Canadian semi-official air stamps, are to some extent boycotted by aerophilatelists.

Western Canada Airways began operations in March 1927 between Rolling Portage, Gold Pines and Red Lake, initially using the stamps of the other companies in this area but introducing their own 10c stamps in July of that year. This airline was notable for issuing the only commemorative airmail stamp in Canada—a 10c celebrating the Jubilee of Canadian Confederation (1867-1927) showing old and new aeroplanes. Various flights in the region north of Winnipeg were carried out by this airline in the period down to February 1930. Yukon Airways also began operations in 1927 with flights between White Horse, Mayo Landing and Dawson. This service was extended in 1928-9 to include Champagne, Telegraph Creek, Carcross and Atlin. This airline had a 25c blue stamp featuring a high-wing monoplane. British Columbia Airways made a brief appearance in 1928, operating flights between Victoria and Vancouver. On the inaugural flight, on 23 July, ordinary Canadian stamps were used, since the Company's special airmail issue was not ready. On 3 August, however, the distinctive 5c stamps, showing an aeroplane over the Straits of Vancouver, were introduced. Further north Klondike Airways inaugurated their airmail service with a flight on 13 October 1928 from White Horse to Dawson via Wernecke, Keno Hill and Mayo Landing. Klondike's 25c blue stamp, showing an aeroplane, was issued in strips of four.

Commercial Airways, operating in the Edmonton-Fort McMurray district of Alberta, between May 1929 and the end of February 1931, issued a number of 10c stamps in various colours. The design of these stamps showed an aeroplane over a map of Alberta, with the various air routes indicated. Two types of the 10c in black are noted; inscribed either VIA AIR or AIR FEE. The Cherry Red Airline also commenced flights in 1929, with various routes to and from Prince Albert, and issued a 10c black and red stamp showing an aeroplane over a lake scene. Maritime and Newfoundland Airways, operating between Newfoundland and the Canadian maritime provinces, issued

20c stamps printed in black and red, or red alone, on yellow paper. A special stamp, intended for company official mail, was printed in black on silver-surfaced paper.

The last of the Canadian airlines to produce its own stamps was Canadian Airways whose distinctive 10c blue and orange stamps appeared in December 1932 for use on the mail carried on the inaugural flight between Edmonton and Fort McMurray. Originally this stamp bore no figures of value but in July 1934 it was reissued with a 10c overprint. The stamp depicted a large low-winged monoplane flying over a city. In lieu of a value this stamp was inscribed with the weight limit per letter ONE OZ.

Some of these companies folded up and vanished without trace; others were amalgamated with their more powerful rivals. Thus the Elliott-Fairchild service was taken over by Patricia Airways which, in turn, was merged with Canada Airways. Commercial Airways was amalgamated with Western Canada Airways. British Columbia Airways ceased operations in tragic circumstances in 1928 when their only aeroplane, with the entire staff on board, was lost in fog on a flight to Seattle. Gradually the Canadian authorities rationalised their airmail services, terminating the contracts to the small companies and instituting their own regular services which eventually covered the country. The government airmail rate was increased from 2 to 3 cents in 1928 and the opportunity was then taken to issue a special airmail stamp. The first design showed an aeroplane over the globe, but this was superseded in December 1930 by a 5c stamp showing Mercury and the globe. In February 1932 the airmail rate increased to 6c and a provisional surcharge was made pending the production of stamps of that value. These 5 and 6c stamps prepaid the Canadian internal air rate and it is interesting to note that over a period of 40 years the rate has risen only slightly: to 7c in 1943 and to 8c in 1964.

Numerous mail flights were made in Canada in the twenties, but the majority of these were more in the nature of stunts and had little or no commercial significance. In May 1928, however, regular air communication between Ottawa and Montreal was established and covers flown on that occasion bore the cachet THIS MAIL WAS CARRIED BY POSTAL AEROPLANE TO MONTREAL. The first major breakthrough in the development of Canadian internal airmails, however, was the inauguration of the Toronto-Montreal service on 22 September 1928. Letters carried on this flight were franked with the special 5c air stamp. On 1 October this service was officially established, with daily flights between the two cities (Sundays excepted). From December 1928 onwards the network of Canadian internal air routes was gradually extended until it covered the whole country. The inaugural flights were, in every case, marked by the use of special cachets on covers bearing the 5 or 6c air stamps. These cachets were invariably pictorial in design and an attractive collection can be formed of the various covers flown, several hundred different cachets having been used in the 20-year period from 1928 onwards.

Great Britain

Before the First World War internal airmails in Britain had been largely sponsored by newspapers, commercial concerns and private individuals, the notable exception having been the Coronation Aerial Post of 1911. No attempt was made, however, to explore the possibilities of regular air services until after the war, but as early as February 1919 an experimental flight was made between London and Edinburgh at the behest of the Air Ministry. During that year there were numerous newspaper flights, but the first mail flights did not materialise till the end of September, and then only because circumstances made this method imperative. During the week from 29 September to 6 October Britain was paralysed by a national strike of rail-workers and rail communications came to a virtual standstill. Serious delays in the delivery of long-distance mail were encountered and, in order to overcome the problem, mail and parcels were conveyed during that week by aeroplane. Letters and parcels are known to have been flown from Kenley to New-castle (29 September) by RAF planes; no surcharge was made and no cachet identifying such mail as carried by air was struck. Flights by private companies were made between Leeds and London and between Barrow and Sheffield and London. Mail carried on the former flight was endorsed with a cachet THE NORTH SEA AERIAL NAVIGATION CO LTD LEEDS. Between 1-6 October an official government air service was operated between London and Bristol, Birmingham, Manchester, New-castle, Glasgow and other large cities. A special air fee of 2s per ounce was levied on letters carried on these flights.

The mail flights during the railway strike were highly successful, but once the emergency was over no further attempt was made to exploit aviation for mail transportation. It was not until April 1923 that the General Post Office began experimental flights, originally with the intention of speeding up the delivery of incoming American mail. Official correspondence, in OHMS covers, is known to have been flown between the cities involved in these flights—London, Plymouth, Manchester, Belfast and Glasgow. Between 1 May and 2 June 1924 an experimental airmail service was operated between Belfast and Liverpool, a special air fee of a halfpenny being raised on each letter. Experiments in expediting the American mail continued in the summer of 1924 but little or no external mail was carried.

The greatest impetus to the development of British internal airmails came in 1926 when the General Strike seriously affected the surface handling of mail between 4 and 12 May. Ordinary and official correspondence was flown by RAF aeroplanes from London over seven different routes, and copies of the government-sponsored newspaper, *British Gazette*, were distributed by the RAF to outlying parts of the country. Seven years elapsed before the lessons learned by the Strike were implemented. Then, appropriately, it was the railway companies who began to diversify their interests by establishing air services. In 1933 the Great Western Railway inaugurated an airmail service between Cardiff and Plymouth. The earliest flown covers bore the company's Newspaper Parcel stamp to denote the payment of the 3d air fee. This service aimed at expediting the mail which was posted on arrival at Cardiff or Plymouth in the usual way. At first this was done without the permission of the postal authorities but subsequently they allowed the Great Western Railway to issue a special airmail stamp. The GWR Air Service was a commercial failure and the company lost about £6,000 before calling a halt to the venture in September 1933. Despite this conspicuous lack of success other airlines began operating services in the same period. International Airlines Ltd (August-September), their successors, Provincial Airways Ltd (November 1933) and Portsmouth, Southsea and Isle of Wight Aviation Ltd (February 1934) operated airmail services in the south-west of England and issued distinctive stamps.

In March 1934 the four major railway companies (LMS, LNER, GWR and Southern Railways) formed the Railway Air Service which began mail flights in August of that year. The special airmail fee of 3d was denoted by means of a rubber stamp, with RAS in a circle and 3D PAID below. The mail contract with this service was shortlived and in November 1934 it was transferred by the Post Office to Hillman Airways. The Railway Air Service, however, had a mail contract between December 1935 and February 1936 and covers bearing the rubber stamped charge mark are known from this period. A subsidiary of the Railway Air Service, known as Great Western and Southern Air Lines, operated airmail flights between the Isles of Scilly and Penzance in the autumn of 1939, mainly for the convenience of troops stationed in the islands at the outbreak of war. In 1934 Captain E. E. Fresson pioneered air routes in the north of Scotland, linking Aberdeen, Inverness, Wick, Orkney and Shetland. He was awarded Post Office contracts to carry mail and though normally such correspondence was not specially marked, various souvenir covers and labels were produced in connection with inaugural flights. Fresson and his competitors eventually amalgamated to form Scottish Airways which operated a special Air Letter Service, in addition to its ordinary postal commitments in 1945-6. These air letters were endorsed with a circular cachet to denote payment of the 4d special handling charge. Scottish Airways and Great Western and Southern Air Lines were taken over by British European Airways in February 1947. Increasing amounts of mail in the ensuing years were carried by BEA aircraft and nowadays this has become the rule rather than the exception. Special air letter stamps have been issued by BEA since 1951 for use on letters handed in at one airport for transmission to another aerodrome where they are then handed over to the Post Office for onward carriage to their destination by surface means. This method is used to speed up the handling of urgent letters. The first three stamps, released in January 1951, were in denominations of 6d, 11d and 1s 4d; subsequently the rates increased progressively until 1961 where they have been pegged (at the time of writing) at 1s, 1s 8d and 2s 7d.

Colombia

In 1920 Colombia became the first country in Latin America to establish a commercial airmail service and to this day it can boast of the most sophisticated network of air routes in that continent.

To understand why Colombia should have taken so enthusiastically to aviation it is important to study the geography of the country. Situated on the north-western side of the South American land mass, with the Pacific on the western side and the Caribbean Sea on the north, Colombia was cut off from the rest of South America by the great mountain ranges and tropical rain forests of the interior.

The Andes are split into three major mountain ranges which divide Colombia and make surface communications extremely hazardous. As late as the end of the last century it used to take several weeks by river boat, railway and lake steamer to travel from Cartagena on the coast (the former Spanish Main) to the capital, Bogota, situated on a high inland plateau. The air services pioneered in 1919 and 1920 instantly reduced this to a flight of less than 30 hours and today it is but a short hop of about an hour's duration.

Difficult communications hampered the political and economic development of Colombia. Collectors are no doubt familiar with the numerous separate issues of stamps made by the various Colombian states; these states were loosely federated and though their powers were considerably curtailed in the 1880s, it was not until the end of the civil war of 1902-3 that Colombia was effectively united. Even then the problems of communication remained to hinder economic growth despite the enormous natural assets of Colombia (it is, for example, the world's leading producer of mild coffee and emeralds, the second largest producer of platinum and ranks among the largest producers of gold, oil, sugar, tobacco and bananas in the world).

With such natural resources it can be imagined that the geographical disadvantages of Colombia were a constant source of frustration to commercial and business interests, and it explains the readiness with which air services were adopted and expanded.

In June 1919 an American flyer named Knox Martin paid a visit to Colombia and organised the first mail flight in that country. Using a Farman biplane, dubbed *Cartagena*, Martin made a short flight from Barranquilla to Puerto Colombia, carrying a small quantity of mail. For the occasion the postal authorities had overprinted two sheets (200 stamps) of the contemporary 2 centavos definitive stamp IER SERVICIO POSTAL AEREO 6-18-19 in five lines. About 160 covers bearing this stamp were flown on 18 June. Since the printing press was too small to overprint a whole sheet at one operation, the sheets were cut up by guillotine into strips of ten and overprinted one row at a time: this accounts for the fact that many of the stamps are found with trimmed perforations. The fifth stamp in each strip had Arabic numerals instead of Roman numerals for the figure 1. Since only 20 of this variety can possibly exist it is a major rarity. Two strips of three and three pairs showing this variety are known in unused condition. Of the 160 covers all but one were addressed to Vicente Puccini, postmaster of Puerto Colombia, or his friend Vicente Lombardi. The only 'non-philatelic' cover from this flight is now in the Fitzgerald Collection at the British Museum.

The success of this flight led to the formation, on 28 September 1919, of Colombia's first commercial airline. At the store kept by Alejandro Echevarria in Medellin on that date the inaugural meeting of shareholders was held to form the Compagna Colombiana de Navegacion Aerea, with an initial share capital of 500,000 gold pesos. Two Farman biplanes, F-40 and F-60, were purchased and Rene Bazin and Jacques Jourdanet, veterans of the First World War, were hired to pilot them. The first regular airmail contract with the government was negotiated in December 1919 and operations began the following February, the first mail flight, between Cartagena and Barranquilla, taking place on the 22nd. The CC de NA (as this company is usually known) suffered many setbacks, due to inadequate aircraft and the rugged terrain over which it operated. Two of its three pilots were killed in crashes early in 1920 and in 1922 it went into voluntary liquidation.

During its comparatively short life, however, the CC de NA produced a wealth of philatelic material. The first stamps used to prepay the airmail charges consisted of publicity labels for Curtis Co overprinted with the name of the air company and surcharged PORTE AEREO $0.10. These curious stamps were used on mail carried between 22 February and 4 March 1920. Six of the nine different labels are known with a 30 centavos surcharge, used on FDCs and these are now very rare.

These stamps were superseded by a 10c stamp lithographed by C. Valiente M of Barranquilla in sheets of 72. An imperforate proof sheet in damaged condition is preserved in the British Museum collection. The first setting of these stamps consisted of 72 stamps in 18 blocks of four stamps; each of the four stamps differs from the others in minute details. A second setting consisted of 68 stamps comprising 34 pairs. The peculiar layout of the subjects in the sheets of the second setting resulted in a *tête-bêche* pair. Two different designs were used for these stamps and they were printed in alternate rows throughout the sheet in both settings. In November 1920 these 10c stamps were surcharged 30c with a violet handstamp while, in the following month, a 20c surcharge was carried out by typewriter. What with shades, se-tenant pairs, *tête-bêche* varieties and errors and variations in the surcharges, not to mention flown covers, the stamps of the CC de NA are both complicated and expensive.

In December 1919 a group of Colombian and German businessmen met in Barranquilla to form a new air company, the Sociedad Colombo-Alemana de Transportes Aereos—better known, from its initials, as SCADTA. Where the French concessionaires of the CC de NA had failed SCADTA triumphed, eventually extending their operations far beyond Colombia. The German company first carried out a thorough survey of the country, studying in minute detail its geography and weather conditions before choosing aircraft most suitable for the purpose. Finally they selected Junkers all-metal hydroplanes, the first of which was delivered in July 1920.

During the summer of 1920 various experimental flights were made between Barranquilla and Girardot on the upper reaches of the Maddalena, where there was a rail link with Bogota. Eventually planes made the flight direct from Barranquilla to Bogota, their engines having been modified for operation at high altitude in the tropics. Regular airmail flights did not actually commence until September 1921, although stamps were issued as early as 4 October 1920 for use on the experimental flights. The first air stamps, lithographed by Valiente in sheets of 48, showed a Junkers seaplane over the Maddalena river, with a paddle-steamer (representing the old method of communications) in the foreground. Each stamp in the sheet differed from its fellows in minor details, so that the stamps can be plated fairly easily—given an unlimited amount of money! Two denominations, 30c and 50c, were issued.

In September 1921 the company extended its services from Girardot to Neiva, hitherto approachable only by a four-day mule ride. A 10c charge was levied on letters from Girardot to Neiva and the 50c stamps were accordingly surcharged VALOR 10 CENTAVOS by handstamp, three different types being used. Inverted or double surcharges are recorded.

A typewritten surcharge of 10c on 50c was also produced about this time, on the initiative of Dr Beyr-Heyder, and although this provisional is known on flown covers, all of these bear his name and address. Experts are, therefore, divided regarding the status of this provisional. SCADTA were not bothered—they had already collected 50c for each of the stamps used by Beyr-Heyder! He was also responsible for a 30c surcharge on 50c stamps, produced in typewriting.

An official 30c surcharge was issued in October-November 1921, due to a shortage of this denomination which was delayed at the printers. Four different types of handstamp were used for this purpose and, as before, errors and varieties are numerous. Various surcharges of 30c were released at Barranquilla, Girardot and Bogota at the end of 1921 and all are scarce, particularly on flown cover.

In November 1921 Valiente produced 10c and 15c stamps and changed the colour of the 30c stamp from black on rose to rose on white paper. Both types of the 30c have been recorded bisected and used as 15c stamps, to prepay the rate between Barranquilla and Cartagena.

The best known of the SCADTA stamps made their debut in December 1921 and remained in use for eight years. The centavo denominations were in an upright format and showed an aircraft over the Maddalena river with the snow-capped volcano of Tolima in the background. The peso values, in a large horizontal format, depicted the main square of Bogota, the Plaza Bolivar, with the Cathedral in the centre and the mountains of Guadeloupe and Montserrate in the background. The denominations were 5, 10, 15, 20, 30, 50 and 60 centavos and 1, 2, 3 and 5 pesos. A new printing of these stamps, from redrawn designs, was made in 1923. The redrawn versions differ from the originals in two major points: in the centavos denominations the aircraft is shown with floats instead of wheels, while in the peso values a small chapel is shown on the left-hand mountain instead of on the right-hand mountain, as erroneously depicted on the original printing.

Both printings were overprinted with a large R for registered mail. In addition the SCADTA stamps of 1921-8 were overprinted with various capital letters, to indicate the consular offices at which these stamps could be purchased, so that senders of letters from abroad could prepay the Colombian internal air-mail postage for the onward transmission of their letters to addresses in the country. The stamps were overprinted with a large capital, the initial of the country in which the agency was located. This was done for several reasons: as a check on the stamps sold by the individual agencies, as a precaution against currency speculation and for statistical purposes.

The overprints were as follows: A (Alemana = Germany), E (Espana = Spain), EU (Estados Unidos = United States), F (Francia = France), GB (Gran Bretaña = Great Britain), P (Panama), S (Suiza = Switzerland), V (Venezuela). Subsequently H (Holland) and I (Italy) were issued. These stamps may be found overprinted in black, violet or red, though all three colours were not used for all the overprints. In addition postal stationery, consisting of envelopes with printed 50c stamps, was issued. These envelopes were issued from the SCADTA office in Berlin, which explains the fact that the inscriptions on them are in German.

Originally the SCADTA stamps had to be applied to the covers of letters and then inserted inside another envelope bearing the stamps of the country of posting. The outer envelopes were removed at Barranquilla and the letters in the inner envelope were then forwarded to the recipient. This two-cover system was inconvenient and eventually Colombia negotiated postal agreements with the countries which had SCADTA agencies, so that the company's stamps could be affixed to the outer envelope, alongside the stamps of the country of the sender. Only Germany, Switzerland, the USA, Holland and Great Britain permitted this mixed franking.

The original series of ten overprints noted above were applied by handstamp. Subsequently machine overprints differing radically from the handstamps were applied to the stamps used at the larger agencies. At the same time the range of overprints increased as SCADTA opened new offices in other countries. The initials found on these stamps are: A-U (Argentina-Uruguay), B (Belgium), BO (Bolivia), BR (Brazil), C (Cuba), CA (Canada), CH (Chile), CR (Costa Rica), D (Denmark), PE (Peru), SU (Suecia = Sweden).

In 1926 the company made further efforts to simplify mail handling by arranging for the Colombian inland fee to be pre-paid in the stamps of the country of the sender and gradually, as these schemes came into effect, the need for the consular overprints died out. They lingered on in some cases as late as 1934, though overprints of this sort did not appear on stamps actually issued after 1928.

A new series appeared in 1929. The centavo stamps depicted the Maddalena river and Tolima mountain as before, but in a smaller format and a new frame design. The peso denominations, however, featured the *Santa Maria*, flagship of Christopher Columbus. The initials of the company appeared as before, but the inscription SERVICIO BOLIVARIANO DE TRANSPORTES AEREOS (Bolivarian Service of Air Transport) indicated a desire to infer that the service extended beyond Colombia to include the other 'Bolivarian' countries (i.e. those liberated from Spanish rule by Simon Bolivar—Bolivia, Ecuador, Panama, Peru and Venezuela). The stamps also included the inscription SOBRETASA AEREA (Air Charge) to denote the payment of the special airmail fee. The series was designed by Miss Dorothea Suffrian and produced at the Government Printing Works in Berlin.

These stamps, inscribed in centavos and pesos, were intended for internal use, but at the same time another series consisting of numerals in a circular frame was produced for use at the various consulates and SCADTA offices abroad. The values were inscribed in centavos and pesos O/M (oro americano = American gold, i.e. US gold dollars). This general foreign issue is usually found on covers with stamps of various foreign countries.

The internal SCADTA series of 1929 was overprinted in December 1930 to mark the centenary of the death of Simon Bolivar. The overprinting was carried out locally and inevitably it bristled with errors and varieties.

In December 1931 the Colombian government declared airmail services a state monopoly and the Administracion del Correo Aereo de Colombia—usually abbreviated to ADELCA was formed. The service continued to be performed by SCADTA under the auspices of ADELCA and the transitional nature of the Colombian airmails of this period is reflected in the use of the SCADTA stamps overprinted CORREO AEREO.

Although the SCADTA stamps rank as locals of a private nature, it is interesting to note that specimens of the overprints of 1932 were sent to the Universal Postal Union and can therefore be regarded as official government issues. As such they are listed in Gibbons, Scott and the other standard catalogues. These overprinted stamps remained in use until May 1933, though they were superseded by a series of Colombian air stamps in August

1932. They were printed in photogravure in Berlin and featured natural products of Colombia, from bananas to emeralds.

Henceforward Colombia issued numerous sets of air stamps. Prior to 1959 they were used specifically to prepay airmail postage, and ordinary (surface postage) stamps had to be used in addition to cover surface handling. In 1959-60 all the airmail stamps then in use were overprinted with the word UNIFICADO (unified) inside the outline of an aeroplane. Since then the airmail fee and inland surface postage have been paid by one stamp.

United States

The development of civil aviation in the United States differed from that in Europe. There was little enthusiasm for passenger flying and, as a result, civil airlines did not emerge as they did in the European countries. The immediate postwar years were a lean time for the pilots demobilised after the First World War. A few of them made a precarious living from barnstorming—displays of aerobatics and stunt-flying at country fairs— or bootlegging—flying crates of illicit liquor during the early days of Prohibition. The only alternative was to secure employment with the Post Office Department. The pay was excellent—up to $1,000 a month—but conditions were hazardous and the death rate among airmail pilots in the early twenties was high.

The United States Post Office had introduced mail flights before and during the First World War but from May 1918 they were given fresh impetus and in the ensuing decade gradually developed into a nation-wide network. In May 1918 a series of three stamps was released showing a Curtiss Jenny aircraft. This machine was used extensively for mail carrying in the United States, along with the British De Havilland DH-4. These stamps were in denominations of 6c, 16c and 24c. One sheet of the 24c was discovered with the centre inverted (the stamp being printed in two colours) and examples of this error now rank among the great rarities of aerophilately. The use of special airmail stamps was discontinued in July 1919 when the supplementary fee was withdrawn. A new series of airmail stamps, however, was introduced in August 1923 for use on mail carried by the Trans-Continental Air Line, the mail route spanning the United States. The inaugural flight of this route took place on 21 August from New York to San Francisco via Cleveland, Chicago, Omaha, Cheyenne and Salt Lake City. The return flight was made two days later.

On 15 February 1926 a new system for airmail was devised in the United States. Henceforward the Post Office offered the various aerial routes to outside contractors and in this way the growth of the independent airlines was stimulated. Between 1926 and 1934 over 30 airmail routes were let to private contractors. These contract services were officially known as Contract Air Mail, each CAM being designated by a route number. For the first, and many of the later, flights special cachets and postmarks were used. At each point on the route the town name was altered, and it is therefore possible to form a collection of each route, including inward and outward journeys, amounting to dozens of covers. A complete collection of first flight covers relating to the Contract Air Mail over the past 45 years would be a formidable undertaking. In addition there have been countless covers and cachets in connection with airport dedication ceremonies.

For the changeover to the CAM flights the United States issued a new set of air stamps, consisting of 10c, 15c and 20c showing aircraft crossing the country from east and west. In 1928 the minimum rate for internal airmail was reduced to 5c and a new stamp, featuring the air beacon at Sherman Hill in the Rocky Mountains, was released on 25 July. Between 1930 and 1934 new stamps, in denominations of 5c, 6c and 8c, were issued featuring an airmail pilot's badge. Since then the United States has issued many attractive airmail stamps, often of a commemorative nature, as well as airmail covers and postcards.

Latin America

Although Colombia made the greatest use of airmail and produced the greatest number of stamps, covers and other aerophilatelic material, several other countries in Latin America were quick to adopt aviation as a means of solving their communications problems. On 1 January 1919 the first airmail flight took place in Chile when Clodomiro Figueroa flew from Santiago to Valparaiso, under the auspices of the Aero Club of Chile. Figueroa took off from Santiago race course in his aeroplane *Valparaiso*. Some 539 covers were carried on this flight, franked by a special 5 peso air stamp, produced photographically and bearing a portrait of Figueroa. This stamp was cancelled by a small violet cachet of the Aero Club. The majority of the covers were distributed personally immediately after the flight, but a few were handed over to the postal authorities and posted in the normal way. These covers bore the usual 10 centavos postage stamps of Chile in combination with the Figueroa stamp.

Neighbouring Ecuador's airmail services were pioneered by an Italian air mission in 1920-2. The first flights, between Guayaquil and Cuenca and from Riobamba to Quito, were carried out by the Italian aviator Elias Liut in the biplane *Telegrapho I* and special covers and cachets were produced in each instance. On 10 September 1922 the first flight from Guayaquil to Esmeraldas, via Salinas and Manta, was carried out by the Italians, Campagnoli, Lodi and Ceccovilli and in their honour 200 of the 1 centavo stamp, 1915-7 series, were overprinted by the postal authorities at Guayaquil. The overprint applied to these stamps was so verbose that it could not be accommodated on the surface of the stamp. The stamps had to be affixed to pieces of white paper, on which the overprint was then applied so that it overlapped the stamp on both sides. Thus the stamp, backing paper and overprint constitute this strange airmail stamp, and the complete unit was then attached to the mail, which consisted almost entirely of copies of the Guayaquil newspaper *El Telegrapho*, and postmarked in the normal way. The overprint, applied in small capitals read CORREO HIDRO AERO GUAYAQUIL SALINAS MANTA ESMERALDAS 10 DE SETIEMBRE DE 1922 PILOTO CAMPAGNOLI OBSERVADOR LODI MECANICO CECCOVILLI. Both Chile and Ecuador made a great number of mail flights in the 1920s and 1930s and were prolific issuers of airmail stamps in that period.

As early as 1919 Brazil had made plans for an airmail service linking Pernambuco and Rio de Janeiro. In connection with this projected flight postcards were overprinted CORREO AEREO— HANDLEY PAGE LTD B 900 with the value 530 reis added. The service, however, did not materialise and it was not until 1925 that the first mail-carrying flights were made in Brazil. Between 13 and 15 January 1925 survey flights were carried out by the French Latecoere Company between Rio and Buenos Aires via Montevideo and special envelopes adorned with the Brazilian and Argentinian flags were produced for the occasion. During the ensuing two years survey flights were made by several

34–35 Semi-official stamps used on covers flown at the aviation meetings of La Baule (1922) and Vincennes (1924). Note the Aviation postmark and early airmail etiquette used on the latter

Was Jahrhunderte hoffend erstrebt,
Was das Träumen und Sehnen der Väter,
Staunend hat es die Mitwelt erlebt
Durch den Flug Zeppelins durch den Äther.

Nach der Katastrophe.

Dr. Ing. Graf Zeppelin.

36–37 Novelty postcard, of 1900, produced to raise funds for the rebuilding of a dirigible airship of Count Zeppelin, after fire had destroyed the prototype at Echterdingen. The card shows the airship before and after the catastrophe companies and by March 1927 five different airlines were in operation. Of these the Latecoere Line (Compagnie Generale Aeropostale) did not issue its own stamps but made use of the official Brazilian airmail issues, while the NYRBA company (New York-Rio-Buenos Aires) flew mail between the United States and Argentina and carried Brazilian airmails en route. The other three companies each produced their own stamps and airmail stationery to prepay postage on the mail flown over their routes. The first of these companies to do so was the German-financed Syndicato Condor whose air service was inaugurated in March 1927 between Porte Alegre and Rio Grande via Pelotas. The stamps featured a condor with wings spread over the flag of Brazil. Between that date and November 1930 the Syndicato Condor issued a number of stamps, many of which were intended for use on mail flown on 'feeder' air services connected with the Zeppelin trans-Atlantic flights.

The S.A. Empresa Viaçaõ Aérea Riograndense (usually known by its initials as VARIG) was formed in May 1927 and between that date and June 1934 produced its own stamps. Although the company is still in existence it now uses ordinary Brazilian government-issued stamps. The earliest stamps used by VARIG consisted of the Condor stamps without the original inscription and with name of the other company superimposed. In 1931 a distinctive series featuring Icarus was released. Between 1927 and 1934 VARIG issued no fewer than 54 different stamps.

The last of the Brazilian airlines to issue its own stamps was Empresa de Transportes Aéreos (ETA) which produced a set of stamps for use on mail carried on the route between Rio de Janeiro and Sao Paulo. The activities of this company were short-lived and though unused examples of its stamps are not uncommon those used on flown cover are now rare.

8

The Zeppelin Saga

Before the First World War the Zeppelin airships operated by DELAG (Deutsche Lutfschiffahrts Aktien-Gesellschaft) had proved that they could be used for the carriage of mail as well as passengers, although airmail at this time was confined to souvenirs and mementoes of the flights. No use was made of Zeppelin airships during the war for mail-carrying purposes. On the other hand enormous technical progress was made by the Germans in this period. Zeppelin airships were used extensively for aerial reconnaissance and bombing raids. German factories produced dirigibles at the rate of one a fortnight; all phases of airship construction, operation maintenance and ground handling were improved immeasurably. About 90 Zeppelins were constructed at four factories for service with the German army or navy. While the Allies were able, in the latter stages of the war, to counter the effectiveness of the Zeppelin as an offensive weapon, it cannot be denied that the German rigid airships of 1918 were capable of long flights at high altitude and carrying comparatively large payloads. By 1918 the size of these airships had increased from the prewar maximum of 70,000 cubic feet to 2,400,000 cubic feet, with a top speed of 80 m.p.h., a ceiling of 20,000 feet and a carrying capacity of more than 50 tons.

By the Treaty of Versailles Germany was prohibited from building any more Zeppelins and existing ones were ordered to be handed over to the Allies in part payment of war reparations. In 1920 France, Britain and the United States were all engaged on the development of rigid airships and possessed a material lead over their former enemy. France, however, abandoned her airship programme in 1923, following the loss of the *Dixmude*. Both Britain and the United States persevered with their development of airships for a number of years but ultimately a series of disasters also brought their experimentation in this field to an abrupt end. On the other hand, Germany quickly regained her position in the airship field and by 1930 had outstripped her opponents. Thus Germany emerged in the 1930s as the only nation to exploit the rigid airship on a large scale. The spectacular flights of these airships made a dramatic impact on aerophilately between the wars and even to this day many collectors make a special study of the Zeppelin mails of that period. But before discussing the Zeppelin airmails it is necessary to mention the progress with dirigibles made by other countries in the 1920s.

Great Britain

Compared with Germany, Great Britain made little attempt to develop rigid airships in the years before the First World War. A large Zeppelin-type airship, the *Mayfly*, was irreparably damaged in 1911 before it ever took to the air and, thus discouraged, British manufacturers abandoned rigid construction till the outbreak of the war. During the First World War attempts in this direction were made, with varying success. The breakthrough came in 1916 when the German airship L-33 was shot down in good condition over Essex. This Zeppelin formed the model for the British R-33 and R-34 which were completed shortly after the end of the war. It was the British, not the Germans, who had the honour of making the first transoceanic flight by airship, when the R-34 flew from Scotland to the United States in July 1919. The airship left East Fortune on 2 July and reached Mineola, New York, five days later. A small mail, consisting of 14 letters endorsed PER HMAS R-34, was carried on the outward journey and dropped from the airship over the village of Selmar in Nova Scotia. The packet containing the letters was not discovered until 8 November of that year. Very few of these letters appear to have survived. One cover, recorded by David Field's *Catalogue of Air Mail Stamps* (1934), was endorsed on the reverse: 'This letter was dropped by H.M. Airship R.34 on 5 July 1919 and picked up at Selmar, Hants Co, Nova Scotia by Milton Weldon, on 8 November 1919. Forwarded to Halifax, Nova Scotia by C. S. Waugh, Postmaster.' One other cover is known, believed to be unique, which was carried by the airship right through to its destination. This bears a four-line cachet in mauve ON HMAS R. 34—EAST

FORTUNE/NEW YORK––JULY 1919. An American 2c stamp was added on arrival in the United States and postmarked 7 July for return to Britain.

The R-34 left Mineola on 9 July and reached Pulham, Norfolk, via Clifden, Galway, four days later. On the return flight a comparatively large quantity of mail was carried, officially stated to be 15 pounds in weight. Since a large portion of this consisted of newspapers, however, actual flown letters are thought to have been relatively few. The mail was taken to London where a special postmark was applied to the reverse of the covers. This postmark consisted of a double-ring handstamp inscribed LONDON at the top and 213 at the foot, with the inscription R 3.4. (*sic*) above the date in the centre. Flown covers from the R-34 are now exceedingly scarce. In 1969 a special postmark was sponsored by the Royal Air Force to mark the fiftieth anniversary of the Atlantic crossing and featured the airship in flight.

In the ensuing decade British airship construction proceeded desultorily. In August 1921 the giant R-38, built for the United States Navy, crashed into the Humber Estuary, killing 44 British and American aircrew. This disaster brought the British airship programme to a halt but three years later work began on two airships, the R-100 and R-101, each having a capacity of 5,000,000 cubic feet. Both were completed five years later, the R-100 by the Airship Guarantee Company at Howden and the latter by the Royal Airship Works at Cardington. The R-100, with accommodation for 1060 passengers, was built on a modified Zeppelin design. Its two year life was uneventful, except for a trans-Atlantic flight in July 1930. Under the command of Major G. H. Scott, it left Cardington on 29 July and flew to Montreal, landing there two days later. Only official correspondence was flown, but while in Canada souvenir postcards, stamped with an oval cachet, were carried on demonstration flights. The cachet was inscribed AERODROME––ST HUBERT ––AIRPORT AIR MAIL SERVICE––POST AERIENNE, with the date across the centre. The return flight was carried out between 13 and 16 August. Mail flown on this occasion was marked on the back with a rectangular cachet depicting the airship moored to a masthead, with the inscription R.100––MONTREAL––1930.

On 5 October 1930 the R-101 crashed into a hillside near Beauvais, France, at the beginning of a flight to India. The crew of 46 were killed in the conflagration and as a result of this catastrophe the British government scrapped its airship programme, the R-100 being dismantled the following year.

United States

Although American interest in airships dated from the turn of the century attention was focused mainly on non-rigid 'blimp' balloons and it was not until the end of the First World War that the United States seriously considered rigid airships. Construction of the ZR-1, later named the *Shenandoah*, began in 1919. This airship, completed four years later, was closely modelled on the German Zeppelin L-49. Between 8 and 15 October the *Shenandoah* made a trans-continental flight from Lakehurst, New Jersey, to Seattle, Washington, and back, a voyage of 9,000 miles. A special cachet inscribed U S NAVAL AIR STA LAKEHURST NJ, with the date in the centre, was applied to flown covers. On 3 September 1925 the *Shenandoah* broke into three parts in a storm over Ohio, killing 14 members of her crew of 43. That the death roll was not higher was due to the fact that the *Shenandoah* was filled with helium instead of hydrogen and thus did not burst into flames.

The ill-fated British R-38 had been designated ZR-2 for use by the United States. She followed the ZR-3, built by the Zeppelin company in 1924 and delivered to the United States in payment of war reparations. This airship was subsequently named the *Los Angeles* and proved to be the most successful of the American airships, making 331 flights in seven years before being decommissioned in 1932. On 20 February 1925 the *Los Angeles* flew from Lakehurst to Bermuda and back. Flown covers bore a cachet AIR MAIL SERVICE NEW YORK, NY with the date in the centre. A second round flight took place on 25 April and the same cachet was applied to mail which, on this occasion, bore the Hamilton Bermuda postmark on arrival. The last of the *Los Angeles* mail flights took place later the same month between Lakehurst and Puerto Rico. A circular cachet was applied to mail on this occasion. The American ZRS-4 *Akron* and ZRS-5 *Macon* both met with disaster within a few years of coming into service and after the loss of the latter airship in 1931 America abandoned her rigid airship programme, confining her interests to non-rigid blimps which were employed during the Second World War on naval patrol.

Italy

Most Italian airship construction during and after the First
World War was of the semi-rigid variety, in which Italy became
the world leader. Three Zeppelins were given to Italy at the
end of the war but inexpert handling resulted in the destruction of two of them soon afterwards and Italy never seriously
explored the possibilities of rigid airships. The majority of
Italian airships were of the Forlanini type and it was one of
these, the F6, which made flights from Milan to Venice and
return in July and September 1921. A cachet inscribed POSTA
AEREA—DIRIGIBLE F6 was applied to mail flown in each direction. Only 26 covers were carried on the Milan-Venice flight and
only 15 on the return flight.

In the 1920s Italy developed the N-type of semi-rigid airship under the direction of General Umberto Nobile. On
11 May 1926 the N-1 *Norge*, carrying an expedition headed by
Roald Amundsen, Lincoln Ellsworth and Nobile, left Spitzbergen for the North Pole. The *Norge* passed over the Pole the
following day and continuing its 3,000-mile flight, landed at
Teller in Alaska on 14 May where it was subsequently dismantled. In connection with this flight a private mail was
carried. Letters bearing ordinary Italian stamps were postmarked at Rome on 8 April or were handed direct to the
aviators on their arrival at Spitzbergen where they were postmarked with the date-stamp of Ny-Alesund. When the *Norge*
reached Alaska the postmark of Teller, dated 13 May, was
applied to the covers. An unofficial label, inscribed VOLO TRANS-
POLARE 1926 POSTA AEREA and showing the airship over the
northern hemisphere, was affixed to the front of each cover. On
the outward flight from Rome to Spitzbergen about 300 letters
addressed to various points en route—Cuers Pierrefeu, Pulham,
Oslo, Leningrad and Vadso—were carried on to King's Bay,
Spitzbergen, from where they were mailed in the ordinary way.

The fourth of the N-type dirigibles was the ill-fated *Italia* in
which Nobile made a second polar flight in May 1928. A small
quantity of the contemporary Italian 1.20 lire airmail
stamp was unofficially overprinted in four lines ESPLORAZIONE
POLARE—NOBILE—DIRIGIBLE ITALIA—1928. These stamps were
used to frank the 62 covers carried by this airship on its polar
mission. Nobile reached the North Pole but on the homeward
flight the airship crashed with a loss of seven lives. Various

rescue expeditions were organised, including those of Roald Amundsen and the Frenchman Guilbaud who never returned. The survivors of the *Italia* were finally located by the Italian airman, Commander Raggazoni, who left Tromso on 6 August 1928 and returned to Italy two days later bringing with him all that remained of the *Italia*'s mail. On these 20 covers a green cachet inscribed ESPLORAZIONE POLARE 1928—RICERCHE DIRIGIBLE ITALIA was applied. The *Italia* affair, and its unpleasant repercussions, signalled the end of airship development in Italy and subsequently Nobile went to Russia where he was for a time engaged in semi-rigid airship design.

Germany

The construction of Zeppelin airships came to a halt temporarily at the end of the First World War but by 1921 the Zeppelin company was back in business, constructing airships for delivery to the Allies. In 1924 the giant LZ-126, later named the *Los Angeles*, was completed and flown across the Atlantic in October of that year. An oval cachet inscribed MIT LUFTSCHIFF ZR 3 BEFÖRDERT (transmitted by Airship ZR-3) was applied to mail carried on this flight. Such covers bore the New York postmark of 15 October.

Four years later the LZ-127 was completed and named the *Graf Zeppelin*, after the pioneer of German airships. This large airship, with a capacity of 3,708,600 cubic feet, took to the air for the first time on 18 September 1928 and made a trial flight over the airship sheds at Friedrichshafen. During the following three weeks the *Graf Zeppelin* made five flights over various parts of Germany, on each of which a cachet, similar to that used for the flights of 1911, was applied to souvenir mail thrown overboard. These cards were postmarked at the various places where the mailbags were subsequently recovered. These preliminary flights were followed by the first double crossing of the Atlantic, for which Germany issued a set of special postage stamps in denominations of 2 marks (postcards) and 4 marks (letters), showing the *Graf Zeppelin* over the northern hemisphere. A special cachet, similar to that used on the Atlantic crossing of the ZR-3, was applied to the mail flown on this occasion. The first Atlantic flight of the *Graf Zeppelin* took place between 11 and 15 October 1928 and the airship flew from Friedrichshafen to New York via Madeira and Bermuda.

The return flight was accomplished between 29 October and 1 November. Mail flown on this occasion was embellished with an elaborate cachet inscribed FIRST FLIGHT AIRMAIL—VIA GRAF ZEPPELIN—UNITED STATES—GERMANY—OCT 28 1928.

During the winter of 1928-9 the *Graf Zeppelin* made nine flights over Germany and souvenir mail was jettisoned as before. These flights were followed by the 'Orientflight' in March 1929, from Germany to Egypt and Palestine via Athens. A pictorial cachet showing the airship over the Pyramids was used on mail carried on this flight. Later in 1929 the *Graf Zeppelin* made flights over south-western Germany and a cruise to Spain and Algeria (April), to Vienna (May) and to New York (August). The return flight to Friedrichshafen was carried out between 8 and 10 August. For all of these flights special cachets were prepared for use on souvenir covers.

Between 15 August and 4 September 1929 Dr Hugo Eckener, Count Zeppelin's colleague and successor, commanded the airship on its famous round the world flight. A distance of 21,700 miles was traversed in 20 days 4 hours. The route taken by the *Graf Zeppelin* on this flight was via Tokyo, Los Angeles and Lakehurst. An elaborate cachet showing the airship in flight round the globe was applied to souvenir mail. This cachet, inscribed FIRST ROUND-THE-WORLD FLIGHT—U.S. AIR MAIL, was used on mail posted in the United States. Special cachets were also prepared at each of the other towns visited, the Tokyo cachet being by far the scarcest. During the latter part of 1929 the *Graf Zeppelin* also made flights to Switzerland (September), Holland (October), the Balkans, Silesia and Spain (October) and Switzerland again (November).

Numerous flights by the *Graf Zeppelin* were carried out in 1930, the most spectacular being the Sudamerikafahrt (South America Flight) which took place between 18 May and 6 June. For this occasion Germany reissued the two Zeppelin stamps of 1928 with the tiny overprint 1 SUDAMERIKA—FAHRT in two lines above the globe. A pictorial cachet showing the airship above a desert scene was struck on souvenir mail. After taking off from Friedrichshafen on 18 May the *Graf Zeppelin* flew via the Cape Verde Islands (where mail was dropped by parachute) to Seville in Spain. At Seville the airship landed and picked up mail for the flight across the South Atlantic to Pernambuco in Brazil. This flight was accomplished in 50 hours on 20-22 May. From Pernambuco the airship flew to Rio de Janeiro (23-25 May) and thence back to Pernambuco (25-27 May). Mail was dropped over Bahia by parachute and then the *Graf Zeppelin* flew on to Havana, Cuba, but owing to bad weather the mail destined for Cuba had to be taken on to the United States. The airship reached Lakehurst on 31 May via Barbados. From Lakehurst the *Graf Zeppelin* crossed the North Atlantic to Seville (2-5 June) and thence to Friedrichshafen on 6 June. For the flight from the United States a set of three Zeppelin stamps was issued and mail was marked with a diamond-shaped cachet inscribed FIRST EUROPE PAN-AMERICA ROUND FLIGHT with a map of the Atlantic showing the route of the airship flights to and from her base. Special Zeppelin stamps were also issued by Argentina, Bolivia and Brazil in connection with the South American flight of 1930, for use on mail taken by aeroplane to Rio de Janeiro or Pernambuco for connection with the airship.

Among the numerous other flights made by the *Graf Zeppelin* in 1930 the most important was that between Friedrichshafen and Moscow in September. Apart from the various special cachets prepared in connection with the Russian flight there were two stamps released by Russia for use on postcards and letter-mail respectively. Later the same month the *Graf Zeppelin* made flights to Switzerland, the Baltic States and to Finland. On the last-named flight Finland released the contemporary 10 mark definitive stamp overprinted ZEPPELIN 1930 in two lines. One stamp in each sheet bore the date error '1830', but the majority of these stamps were detected and destroyed before they could be sold to the public.

During 1931 the *Graf Zeppelin* continued her programme of international flights, several of which resulted in the issue of special Zeppelin stamps by the respective countries visited. Hungary released two stamps in March, Egypt two surcharged air stamps in April, Iceland a set of three overprints in July, Liechtenstein a pair of pictorials in June, and Brazil and Paraguay three stamps each in September.

In July 1931 the *Graf Zeppelin* carried out an ambitious survey flight over the polar regions. The flight was made on 25 July from Friedrichshafen to the Arctic via Berlin, Leningrad and Franz Josef Land and thence back to Friedrichshafen. The highlight of this trip was a survey flight over the Arctic Sea and a visit to the Soviet ice-breaker *Malygin*. For this flight Germany reissued the Zeppelin stamps of 1928 in new colours and denominations overprinted POLAR-FAHRT 1931. Russia issued a set of four stamps, either imperforate or perforated, showing the airship over the *Malygin*, with a Polar bear in the foreground. In addition there were several fancy cachets applied to mail posted at Friedrichshafen and Leningrad while even the ice-breaker *Malygin* had a special cachet inscribed in French.

In March-April 1932 the *Graf Zeppelin* made her third great South America flight, from Friedrichshafen to Rio and Pernambuco. An even larger number of covers and souvenir cachets was prepared on this occasion than had appeared for the previous flights to Latin America, but only Paraguay issued special stamps, a set of five triangulars being released on 17 March. Unsold remainders of these stamps were subsequently overprinted to celebrate New Year 1933.

In 1933 the *Graf Zeppelin* made no fewer than nine South American round flights, all of which resulted in a plethora of special covers, cancellations and cachets. Paraguay issued a further set of five Zeppelin stamps in May 1933 in connection with the first of the return flights. Italy and her colonies, Cyrenaica and Tripolitania, issued Zeppelin stamps in May 1933. The ninth South American flight of 1933 took place in October. From Rio de Janeiro the *Graf Zeppelin* flew on to Miami, Akron and Chicago in connection with the Century of Progress World's Fair then being held in that city. From Chicago the airship returned to Friedrichshafen across the North Atlantic. For this flight Germany reissued the 1, 2 and 4 mark Zeppelin stamps, this time overprinted CHICAGOFAHRT— WELTAUSSTELLUNG 1933 (Chicago flight—World Fair). The United States produced a 50c airmail stamp on this occasion, featuring the *Graf Zeppelin* between the Chicago Exposition building and the airship hangar at Friedrichshafen.

In its first five years in service the *Graf Zeppelin's* international flights accounted for almost a thousand different souvenir covers, postcards, cachets, postmarks and stamps. Though comparatively few souvenirs appeared during her last four years in operational service, this famous airship chalked up the remarkable record of 590 flights, including 144 ocean crossings, and had flown 1,053,391 miles carrying 13,110 passengers and 235,300 lb of mail and freight. The *Graf Zeppelin* was decommissioned in 1937.

Her successor, the LZ-128, did not get beyond the drawing board, but in 1936 the stupendous LZ-129 *Hindenburg*, with a capacity of 7,063,000 cubic feet, was completed. This 803-feet long airship was powered by four 1,100 h.p. Mercedes engines and had a range of almost 9,000 miles at a cruising speed of 78 m.p.h. In 1936 this airship operated the first truly commercial air service across the North Atlantic by carrying 1,002 passengers on ten scheduled trips between Germany and the United States, the eastbound crossings averaging 65 hours and the westbound crossings 52 hours. Germany issued two stamps in March 1936 depicting the *Hindenburg* in flight over the North Atlantic. On 6 May 1937, while landing at Lakehurst on the first of her 1937 season flights, the hydrogen-inflated *Hindenburg* was ignited by static electricity in the atmosphere, and burst into flame. The airship was completely destroyed with the loss of 36 lives—the first passenger fatalities in the history of commercial aviation. The LZ-130, christened *Graf Zeppelin*, was completed and tested in September 1938. Designed for helium operation this sister ship of the *Hindenburg* was built for the North Atlantic service, but the tense international situation at the time, and the refusal of the United States to export the helium required, prevented this airship being brought into service. Subsequently the *Graf Zeppelin* was modified for hydrogen operation but its use was confined to demonstration flights over Germany and it saw neither commercial nor military service. German airship construction came to an end in July 1939 and in April the following year the LZ-130 and her namesake, the old LZ-127, were dismantled and the scrap steel and aluminium from their hulls used for the Nazi war effort. In July 1944 Allied bombing raids on Friedrichshafen destroyed the airship hangars and installations. The destruction of the Zeppelin Luftschiffbau works during the Second World War undoubtedly saved the Zeppelins from the ignominy of neglect and decay in the postwar years. Developments in trans-oceanic, heavier-than-air machines during and after the war would have rendered the airships obsolete in any event. In their heyday, in the twenties and thirties, however, the airships, and particularly the Zeppelins, captured the imagination of the world and they are fondly remembered today by the astonishing wealth of souvenirs engendered by their flights.

9

The Development of
Commercial Airlines

The First World War had demonstrated the practicability of aircraft and proved that what had been regarded as a sport or entertaining novelty had serious applications. The trail-blazers of the twenties, in turn, proved that aeroplanes were capable of making flights covering thousands of miles and spanning the oceans. It only remained for this experience to be converted to commercial use. Civil aviation on a commercial basis emerged as soon as the First World War was over. In the early twenties numerous small companies emerged briefly, operating one or two reconditioned wartime aircraft, and disappeared after a short time, either going bankrupt or being merged with their larger rivals. While aeroplanes retained their novelty the embryonic airlines were able to eke out a precarious existence by giving joy rides or aerobatic demonstrations at fairs and carnivals. But when the novelty wore off many of these small companies found that there was insufficient passenger or freight traffic all year round to justify their existence. In Britain the problem of the small companies was solved to some extent by their amalgamation to form larger organisations. In this way, for example, British Marine Air Navigation, Daimler Airways, Handley Page Transport and Instone Air Lines came together in March 1924 to form Imperial Airways Ltd. This grandiose title was hardly justified at the time, since the scale of operations was fairly limited. In its first year this company operated flights from London to Paris, Brussels, Amsterdam, Berlin, Cologne and the Channel Islands—in most cases at only weekly intervals. But within a few months several of these services had become daily and the range of flights was increased to cover Zurich in Switzerland.

At the same time Imperial Airways was keenly concerned with the development of long-range routes which would eventually cover the British Commonwealth. In 1921 experimental flights were carried out by the Royal Air Force between England, Cairo and Baghdad in Iraq. On the first of these flights, which left England on 4 August, only one official letter was carried. On 21 August the first formal arrangement for the transmission of mail (official correspondence only) was made and on 13 October the service was extended to the general public. Mail flown on that occasion was endorsed BY AIR CAIRO —BAGHDAD and a special charge of 1s per ounce was levied. This fortnightly service, originally performed by Royal Air Force planes, was taken over by Imperial Airways in December 1926. The first aircraft, the Handley Page biplane *City of Baghdad,* left Croydon on 18 December carrying an unofficial mail of eight letters. Some of these letters were afterwards flown from Cairo to East Africa on an experimental flight in February 1927.

In 1926 Imperial Airways had completed preparations for an extension of the air service from Baghdad to Basra and thence down the Persian Gulf to India. The survey flight which mapped out the England-India route took place between 27 December and 8 January 1927, with Sir Samuel Hoare and Sir Sefton Brancker as passengers. The company was beset with a number of problems in the early years of this route. It was not until 1929 that an agreement could be reached with the Persian government over the question of flights over the Gulf area. The first through service of airmail from London to Karachi was inaugurated on 30 March 1929. Souvenir envelopes in red were prepared by Imperial Airways for this occasion and flown from Croydon via Athens, Alexandria, Gaza, Baghdad, Basra, and Jask to Karachi. Commemorative cachets were applied to mail despatched from Gaza and Baghdad. Airmail rates varied from 2½d per ½oz for letters destined for Egypt and Palestine to 6d per ½oz for the Gulf ports and India. On the return flight mail from India was given a circular cachet BY AIR and a quantity of mail despatched from Iraq, Palestine and Greece, en route bore souvenir cachets. Significantly the Italian government refused to permit Imperial Airways flights over their territory and the aircraft had to make a considerable detour. Mail was carried by air as far as Basle and then went by train to Genoa; from Genoa the mail was flown by a circuitous route to Athens. In November the route was modified so that mail could be flown all the way. The aircraft now flew via Cologne, Nuremberg, Vienna, Budapest, Belgrade and Salonica. At the other end the service was extended from Karachi to Jodhpur and Delhi in December 1929. A special cachet was applied to mail carried on the Karachi-Delhi leg and also on the return flight. The small rectangular cachet depicted two biplanes and was inscribed AIR MAIL KARACHI-DELHI FIRST FLIGHT.

In April 1930 the London-Karachi service was accelerated from seven and a half days to six and a half days by cutting down the portion travelled by rail. A year later experimental extensions of the London-Karachi service were made, eventually linking Karachi to Australia via Calcutta, Akyab and Rangoon (Burma), Penang and Singapore (Straits Settlements), Batavia (Dutch East Indies) and Darwin. The mails were then transshipped and flown by QANTAS aircraft to Melbourne. Covers flown on these experimental flights, identifiable by their postmarks and often embellished with souvenir cachets and the autographs of the pilots, are of great interest and value to aerophilatelists. Cachets of a similar nature were employed on other extensions of the service, such as the first Burma-Australia mail flight (April 1931), Karachi-Calcutta (July 1933) and Rangoon-London (October 1933).

Continued trouble with the Persian authorities was resolved in October 1932 when Imperial Airways established an alternative air base at Bahrein in the Persian Gulf. Special covers inscribed FIRST ARABIAN AIR MAIL or ENGLAND-INDIA VIA BAHREIN AND OMAN were printed in honour of the occasion. The Calcutta-Rangoon section of the route came into operation in September 1933; again souvenir covers, showing a map of the route and a suitable inscription, were issued. Although experimental flights to Australia took place as early as 1931 it was not until December 1934 that a regular airmail route all the way from England to Australia could be established. Souvenir covers commemorating the inauguration of this service were produced with the inscription OPENING OF THE AIR MAIL SERVICE BY IMPERIAL AIRWAYS AND QANTAS EMPIRE AIRWAYS BETWEEN ENGLAND AND AUSTRALIA. This cover was printed in red and blue for Imperial Airways and in light blue and black for QANTAS.

Between 1919 and 1929 various experimental flights were made between England and South Africa, and some of them have left their mark in aerophilately. In November 1925 Alan Cobham flew from London to Cape Town via Lyons, Brindisi, Athens, Cairo, Wadi Halfa, Khartoum, Kisumu, Jinja, Pretoria, Johannesburg and Bloemfontein. A special souvenir card, giving a full description of the machine and the route followed, was prepared by Imperial Airways and sanctioned by the British Postmaster-General. Only four complete sets of these cards, posted at various places en route, are known. Between 4 and 13 October 1930 Lieutenant Caspareuthus made an experimental flight from London to Cape Town. Only 25 letters were carried on this flight and no special cachet or postmark was employed.

In February 1931 Imperial Airways carried out the first leg of their proposed London-Cape route, with a flight from London to Mwanza in Tanganyika. On this occasion Imperial Airways produced no fewer than three different covers. The first, known to collectors as the 'Rising Sun' variety, was intended for official greetings only and is comparatively rare. The covers sold to the public bore a silhouette map of Africa with the inscription BY IMPERIAL AIRWAYS—FIRST AIR MAIL. ENGLAND-AFRICA or EGYPT-EAST AFRICA appeared in the bottom line, the latter form being used on covers mailed on the last stage of the route. Various cachets were applied to the covers en route. On the return flight, inaugurated on 10 March, official cachets were applied at Juba, Khartoum, Wadi Halfa, Malakal, Kosti, Luxor, Assiut and Assouan. The second leg of the London-Cape route was scheduled for January 1932 but in the preceding November it was decided to make the first flight on 9 December in order to carry the Christmas mail to South Africa. Covers with a Springbok motif were produced on this occasion. Special cachets were applied to mail at various stopping places in the Sudan and Rhodesia. The mail arrived at Cape Town on 21 December. For the full inauguration of the service, on 20 January 1932, similar covers but with the Imperial Airways 'speedbird' motif substituted for the Springbok were used. Passengers as well as mail were carried on the route as far as Nairobi in Kenya; for the rest of the route mail only was flown. Mail was picked up at most of the stopping places and, in addition, mail from a number of European centres and India was picked up en route. Special cachets in connection with this flight were applied to mail at Athens, Assiut, Assouan, Mpika, Salisbury and Bulawayo. The mail arrived in Cape Town on 2 February 1932. The first feeder service opened in connection with this route was from Windhoek in South West Africa to Kimberley and special postmarks were provided for use on mail flown on this occasion. Subsidiary services were organised by Wilson Airways in Central Africa and the Rhodesian and Nyasaland Airways throughout the Rhodesias.

An important spur line to the London-Cape route was that linking Khartoum to Lagos in Nigeria across the Sahara. This route was officially inaugurated on 15 February 1936 when a flight was made from Khartoum to Kano in northern Nigeria, via El Obeid, El Fashar, Geneina, Abecher, Ati, Fort Lamy and Maidugari. Cachets were applied to flown covers at Ati and Abecher. This mail reached Kano on 16 February and a return flight was made the following day. This service was extended to Lagos, via Kaduna, Minna and Oshogbo on 21 October. A special cachet inscribed AIR MAIL—FIRST DESPATCH—LAGOS-LONDON with the date below was applied to mail flown on 29 October 1936 on the first return flight.

In June 1937 Imperial Airways inaugurated its flying boat service from Southampton to Durban, Natal by the *Canopus*. A special silver postmark with an ivory handle was used to impress the cancellation SOUTHAMPTON AERODROME to a handful of letters, addressed to high-ranking South African officials and carried in a silk mailbag. The bulk of the mail carried, however, bore no special postmark and was placed in ordinary mail-bags. The *Canopus* left Southampton on 2 June and flew via Kisumu, Mombasa, Dar-es-Salaam, Lindi, Mozambique, Quelimane, Beira, Inhambane and Lourenço Marques arriving at its destination on 8 June. Simultaneously the flying boat *Courtier* flew from Durban to Southampton following the same route. Later the same month Britain introduced the first Empire Air Mail scheme, permitting letters to be flown to Africa at the 'all-up' rate of $1\frac{1}{2}$d per $\frac{1}{2}$oz. Various Commonwealth countries subsequently participated in this scheme which permitted airmail to be carried at greatly reduced rates. This scheme came to an end on the outbreak of the Second World War when air services were severely curtailed or were withdrawn altogether.

The England-Australia and England-Cape routes operated by Imperial Airways and its subsidiaries between them served a large part of the world. Only the great ocean routes across the Atlantic and the Pacific eluded Imperial Airways for many years. Not until 1937 did Imperial Airways conduct its first survey flights across the Atlantic to explore the commercial feasibility of the route. On 25-26 May the first survey flights were carried out by the flying boat *Cavalier* between Bermuda and New York and return. No mail seems to have been carried on these flights, but a three line cachet was applied to mail flown by this machine on 16 June. A survey flight by the flying boat *Caledonia* was made between Foynes, Ireland, and Botwood, Newfoundland, on 5-6 July, a return flight being carried out on 16 July. Between the beginning of July and the end of September 1937, when the service was discontinued for the winter, ten Atlantic crossings were made by the *Caledonia* and her sister ship *Cambria*. The following year an experimental flight was made from Foynes to New York via Montreal. The flying boat *Maia* carried a small seaplane *Mercury* which was launched on the last stage of the flight. Special airmail editions of certain newspapers—the *Daily Mail, Daily Sketch* and *Daily Herald*—were flown by the *Mercury* to New York.

On 5 August 1939 Britain's trans-Atlantic service was inaugurated by the flying boat *Caribou* between Southampton and New York via Foynes, Botwood and Montreal. Special cachets were produced by the Irish and Canadian authorities for use on mail despatched from their stopping places on both outward and return flights. Imperial Airways never got round to attempting the Pacific crossing. War broke out before the route could be surveyed and the following year the company was transformed into the giant nationalised British Overseas Airways Corporation. Its memory lingered on in a surprising way: the Egyptian airmail stamps current from 1933 to 1947 featured the Imperial Airways airliner *Hannibal* over the Pyramids. This Handley Page machine was lost on 1 March 1940 near Sharjah in Arabia.

KLM

Whereas most of the great airlines of the world developed gradually out of a group of smaller private companies, the Dutch airline KLM (Koninklijke Luchtvaart Maatschappij) enjoyed the full support of the government from its inception. The idea behind KLM was first proposed by a Dutch pilot, Lieut Albert Plesman, who organised a Dutch National Air Exhibition in Amsterdam in August 1919. A syndicate of businessmen were interested in this Exhibition and met shortly afterwards to found an airline. KLM—The Royal Airways Company, to translate its name—came into being in October 1919 and commenced flying operations in May 1920, with the inauguration of the Amsterdam-London service. The first mail contract was awarded to the company in July 1920 and in the ensuing decade the company rapidly expanded until its network of air routes covered western Europe, with flights to Brussels, Paris, Bremen, Hamburg, Copenhagen and Malmö. A set of three air stamps was released by Holland in 1921 but they were discontinued a few months later.

The Netherlands, like Britain, was concerned with finding ways of linking up the mother country with the colonies, particularly the Dutch East Indies, and as early as 1919 a prize of 100,000 guilders (about £10,000) was offered for the first successful flight from Holland to Batavia, and this sum was later increased to 228,000g. A flight to the Indies, however, remained impracticable so long as the British authorities refused permission for aircraft to fly over Iraq. In 1924 these objections were removed and on 1 October of that year the KLM pilot Van der Hoop and two companions took off from Amsterdam for Batavia. After numerous setbacks and delays they eventually reached their destination on 24 November. Some 281 covers were flown by Van der Hoop with a special postmark. Three years later Lieut Koppen made an experimental flight to Batavia and on this occasion 2,092 covers were carried, marked with a special cachet. Both Van der Hoop and Koppen were portrayed on a pair of Dutch airmail stamps issued in 1928. Further trial flights between Amsterdam and Batavia took place in September 1928, the Koppen and Van der Hoop stamps being used on mail flown on this occasion.

During 1929 KLM's services ranged in versatility from local flights to relieve the ice-bound Wadden Islands, services to Switzerland, Austria, Russia and Turkey, and the inauguration of an experimental mail service to the Indies. Local flights in the Indies were started that year by KNILM, a subsidiary of KLM. In 1930 the flights to the Dutch East Indies were put on a regular footing, with a weekly return service, soon afterwards increased to twice weekly. Apart from the airmail stamps and cancellations, special postmarks and cachets were provided for the Christmas flights to the East and West Indies in 1933 and 1934. In the latter year experimental flights from Holland to the Dutch West Indies and Surinam were attempted. A local service linking the islands of Curaçao and Aruba was initiated in January 1935 and this was later extended to cover various points in Venezuela, Trinidad and Colombia. By 1937 KLM had completed its 500th flight to the East Indies and in the years immediately before the Second World War links with the international air routes of other major airlines had been forged.

The last of KLM's prewar routes was that linking Amsterdam to Cape Town. An experimental 'goodwill' flight was carried out in December 1938 in connection with the celebrations marking the centenary of Dingaan's Day—the Boer victory over the Zulus. The KLM aircraft *Reiger* (named after one of Van Riebeeck's ships which discovered the Cape) performed this experimental flight and souvenir covers were flown on this occasion in both directions. The outbreak of the Second World War prevented the development of this route and it was not until 1949 that KLM could resume their service to South Africa. In 1946 KLM inaugurated their service to North and South America with flights in May and December to New York and Montevideo respectively. Special 'first flight' covers were, in each case, carried.

Lufthansa

Although Germany was severely handicapped immediately after the First World War by having to surrender the bulk of her aircraft to the Allies in payment of war reparations, it was characteristic of her aviation industry that, within a few months of the cessation of hostilities, several small aviation companies had started up in a modest way, operating passenger flights between various cities. In the early 1920s these small companies emulated KLM and banded together to form Deutsche Aero Lloyd and Junkers Luftverkehr with government support. In 1926 these two companies amalgamated to form Deutsche Lufthansa. Over the years government control of this airline became more complete and under the Nazi regime it was a fully nationalised airline.

Just as KLM were fortunate in having Anthony Fokker to design their aircraft, so also Lufthansa relied mainly on Hugo Junker whose aeroplanes, with their distinctive corrugated allmetal structure, gave this airline an enviable reputation for reliability. The German companies began operating internal air services in October 1919 and in order to prepay the airmail rates on letters and postcards two stamps were released that month, featuring a winged posthorn and a biplane respectively. The German airmails of the 1920s and 1930s were replete with special airport cachets and postmarks. The cachets, struck on outgoing and incoming mail, usually bore the inscription MIT DER FLUGPOST (or LUFTPOST) BEFÖRDERT (transmitted by the airpost), and the majority of them also incorporated the name of the airport. These airport arrival and departure cachets varied considerably in lettering and appearance.

In July 1924 Germany inaugurated its air service to Turkey and for the occasion mail was franked by a special stamp featuring a Junkers monoplane and inscribed JUNKERS LUFTVERKEHR (Junkers Air Traffic) with BERLIN-ANGORA below. This stamp had a value of 2 gold marks. Later the same year Germany began night flights to Stockholm from Berlin and covers carried on the first flight bore Berlin and Stockholm postmarks. Other routes in Europe were opened up in the period between the wars—to Vienna and Prague (1927), to Königsberg and Moscow via Riga (1927), from Berlin to Rome (1928), from Hamburg to Antwerp (1929), from Breslau to Warsaw (1930), from Berlin to Shanghai, via Moscow, Irkutsk, Manchuria and Peking (1931), from Berlin to Salonika (1932), and many others. From 1928 onwards the Zeppelin company, acting as a subsidiary of Lufthansa, pioneered Atlantic crossings. The flights of the *Graf Zeppelin* and the *Hindenburg* are dealt with in Chapter 8.

Although the Germans pinned their faith mainly on airships for long-range, oceanic flights, they gave serious attention to heavier-than-air machines on the same routes. In 1929 experimental flights were carried out using the giant flying boat Dornier DO-X on Lake Bodensee. Mail was jettisoned on German, Swiss or Austrian territory and subsequently posted in the normal way. Covers were marked with a cachet SUDFUNK AN BORD DO-X (southern transmission on board DO-X), A year later, in November 1930, this great flying boat set out from Friedrichshafen on a flight to South America. The flight was subject to numerous delays and setbacks and stops were made at Amsterdam, Calshot (near Southampton), Bordeaux, Lisbon and the Canary Islands, South America not being reached till June 1931. Covers flown on this epic trip bore a cachet ERSTER UBERSEEFLUG—EUROPA-AMERIKA—DES DORNIER FLUGSCHIFFS DO-X (first overseas flight Europe-America of the Dornier flying boat DO-X).

The best-known flight of this giant flying boat took place in May 1932 when it flew from Newfoundland to Germany, via the Azores and England. In connection with this flight the Newfoundland postal authorities overprinted the $1 air stamp with the inscription TRANS-ATLANTIC WEST TO EAST PER DORNIER DO-X MAY 1932 ONE DOLLAR AND FIFTY CENTS in five lines. A total of 8,000 stamps was thus overprinted and completely sold out on the day of issue, although sales were restricted to four stamps per applicant. Altogether some 1,804 letters were franked with these stamps and carried by the DO-X to Europe.

In September 1933 the DO-X made a flight from Passau to Staad in Switzerland and mail on this occasion bore an appropriate cachet. Subsequently little use could be found for this aircraft which, like the British Princess flying boat 20 years later, proved to be something of a white elephant. At any rate, as a means of long-distance flying, it soon faded from the scene.

Despite the comparative failure of the DO-X the Dornier company managed to develop a flying boat which was more practicable. This was the Dornier Wal which was used effectively on the South Atlantic route from 1933 till 1938 when the service was discontinued. Mail was flown by Heinkel land-planes from Stuttgart to Seville, from Seville to Bathurst in Gambia by Junkers land-plane, from Bathurst to Natal in Brazil by Dornier Wal and from Natal to Buenos Aires by aircraft of the Brazilian Syndicato Condor company. To facilitate the operation of the trans-Atlantic service the Germans made use of several ships anchored in mid-ocean. The flying boat would alight on the sea near the ship and be hoisted on board by crane, for refuelling. After refuelling and pre-flight checks the Wal was moved on to a railway from which it was catapulted off the deck of the ship into the air. By using relays of flying boats (one was always kept in readiness on the catapult ramp) the mails could be transferred from a newly arrived machine and sped on their way. The first experimental flights of the catapult mail took place from the steamer *Westfalen* in 1933 and a regular fortnightly service was inaugurated on 3 February 1934. In August 1934 the steamer *Schwabenland* joined the *Westfalen* and the service was modified by having the ships stationed on the American and African coasts respectively. In 1936 a third vessel, the *Ostmark* was added to the service and this enabled a rota-system to be introduced in order to speed up the trans-Atlantic flight. Unlike the two earlier ships (which were converted cargo vessels) the *Ostmark* was specially constructed for the purpose. The various changes in the South Atlantic service, the inauguration of new routes and stages and the addition of the later ships, all found philatelic record by way of special covers, cachets and postmarks sponsored by Lufthansa and Syndicato Condor.

The activities of Lufthansa were curtailed by the Second World War although tribute to the company was paid by a set of three stamps issued by Germany in 1944 to mark the 25th anniversary of the airline. At the end of the war Lufthansa came to a halt and it was not until 1956 that its services could be restarted. Since then Lufthansa has emerged as one of the world's leading airlines, operating jet services to every part of the globe.

Sabena

Like KLM and Lufthansa the Belgian national airline Sabena can trace its origins back to 1919, the year in which a company entitled Syndicat National pour l'Etude des Transports Aeriens (SNETA) was formed to explore the possibilities of commercial aviation in Belgium and the Congo. Flying began in 1920, with services to Paris and London. Simultaneously local flights were made in the Belgian Congo, the latter country issuing distinctive airmail stamps in 1922. In 1923 the Société Anonyme Belge d'Exploitation de la Navigation Aerienne—usually known from its initials as Sabena—was founded, under the joint ownership of the Belgian government, the major banks and the Congo colonial authorities.

For years the projected Belgium-Congo air route remained no more than a dream, although in 1925 Captain Edmund Thieffry made a flight from Belgium to the Congo and demonstrated the feasibility of the route. During the ensuing years such airmails as linked the Congo with Europe were carried by the French Latecoere company. In May 1930 the Belgians obtained permission to fly over French African territory and in the following December the aviators Van der Linden and Fabry flew from Brussels to Leopoldville and then set off from Leopoldville on a return flight to Brussels. On account of an accident at Fort Lamy (Tchad) the mail had to be forwarded by the ordinary route and ultimately reached Paris on 30 March 1931. A special cachet LIAISON AERIENNE BELGIQUE-CONGO was applied to flown covers.

Meanwhile Sabena was expanding and improving its network of services in Europe. Flights to Hamburg were inaugurated in 1929 and a night service to London began in 1930. In 1935 Sabena linked up with the air routes operated by the French company Regie Air Afrique between Algiers and Brazzaville (French Congo). Eventually the air routes operated jointly by the French company and Sabena spanned the African continent and linked places as far apart as Madagascar and Brussels.

After Belgium was overrun by the Germans in 1940 Sabena's European activities came to an end, but its operations in the Congo continued all through the Second World War and, indeed, assumed new importance as part of the link in the trans-African air routes from Khartoum to Lagos and from Takoradi to Cairo. Towards the end of 1944 Sabena began direct flights from Leopoldville to England via Casablanca and Lisbon and flights from Leopoldville to Brussels began again soon after the liberation of Belgium in 1945.

Sabena inaugurated its postwar trans-Atlantic run in June 1947, the inaugural flight being made in connection with the celebrations attending the unveiling of the American war memorial at Bastogne. Covers franked with the Bastogne Memorial stamps and struck with a souvenir cachet, were flown from the former battlefield direct to New York. Since then Sabena has extended its network of air routes to cover Western Europe, North America and Africa. The inception of each route, and the introduction of new aircraft has been marked in each instance by souvenir 'first flight' covers.

Qantas

The first of the world's major airlines to be formed outside Europe was the Queensland and Northern Territory Aerial Service, better known as Qantas, from the initial letters of the name. Although this company's activities soon extended far beyond the areas specified in its title the original name has been retained to this day. During its first 14 years of existence Qantas concentrated its attentions on developing a network of air routes in northern and eastern Australia but in January 1934 a new company was incorporated, known as Qantas Empire Airways, to develop the overseas routes hitherto flown by Qantas aircraft in conjunction with Imperial Airways. Between 1931 and 1934 Imperial Airways had gradually extended its major route from London to India and down through Malaya to Singapore. Qantas Empire Airways was responsible for developing the route from Singapore to Brisbane which came into operation in December 1934. The first direct airmail from Britain to Australia left London on 4 December and arrived in Brisbane on 21 December. Both Imperial Airways and Qantas produced souvenir covers to celebrate the event. At first Qantas aircraft flew only on the leg from Brisbane to Darwin but in 1935 weekly flights all the way to Singapore were introduced and the following year the service became twice weekly. Flying boats were put on this service in June 1938. In August 1938 the Empire Airway Scheme was applied to the Australia route and all first class mail between Britain and Australia was automatically carried by air, the Australian postage rate being fixed at 5d per half ounce. Souvenir covers marked the inception of a thrice weekly mail flight from Australia to Britain on 9 August 1938. This scheme was suspended for the duration of the Second World War, although Qantas operated airmail flights during the war, from Australia to India via Singapore, until the Japanese invasion of Malaya in December 1941 brought the project to an end. Between that date and February 1942 Qantas aircraft continued to maintain communications between Britain and Australia using the 'Horseshoe Route'—by various devious routes to India to avoid Malaya, and thence by air to Cairo and Cape Town and from there to Britain by sea. During the rest of the war air communications between Britain and Australia were precariously maintained by long-range flights from Western Australia to East Africa or across the Indian Ocean to Ceylon, using Catalina flying boats. From August 1944 onwards special air letter forms were adopted for airmail carried on this route to Australia by Qantas. This service was thrown open to the general public, the previous flights having been restricted to official and military mails. A commemorative overprint was applied to air letters carried on this inaugural flight.

Immediately after the war Qantas began to redevelop its air routes to Britain via Singapore and India. This service became fully operational in April 1946. In the postwar years new services were opened up by Qantas between Australia and New Guinea, New Caledonia, Fiji, Norfolk Island, the New

Hebrides, Hong Kong and Japan, the various first flights being suitably commemorated by special covers, labels and cachets. In November 1948 an experimental flight between Sydney and Johannesburg brought Australia and South Africa closer together. In 1951 flights via the Cocos-Keeling Islands began and in August 1952 the regular service from Sydney to Johannesburg, was instituted. In May 1954 Qantas began operating a regular service across the Pacific, linking Sydney and Vancouver. In the ensuing decade the progressive adoption of larger and more powerful jet-liners has enabled Qantas to fly air routes spanning the globe and, at the present time, this company ranks as one of the world's top ten airlines, in terms of distances covered and passengers, mail and freight carried.

BOAC and BEA

Imperial Airways and British Airways amalgamated in 1939 to form the British Overseas Airways Corporation (BOAC) and began operational flying in April 1940 shortly before the Battle of Britain broke out. BOAC could hardly have had a less auspicious beginning and during its first five years in existence had to struggle against tremendous odds and operate with obsolescent equipment and machines. The entry of Italy into the war on the Axis side put an end to the old Imperial Airways route across Europe to the Middle East and shortly afterwards BOAC inaugurated a new route via Lisbon and the west coast of Africa to Nigeria, whence aircraft flew across the Sahara to the Sudan and linked up with the main Cairo-Durban route. From Durban an air route across the Indian Ocean took the mails to India, Malaya and Australia. Even this circuitous route was curtailed as a result of Japanese occupation of Malaya in 1942.

At the end of the Second World War British air routes were re-organised and British European Airways (BEA) was established in August 1946 to handle domestic and European flights. At the same time British South American Airways was established to operate routes over the east and west coast of South America. BSAA was short-lived, being merged in BOAC in 1949. BOAC found the South Atlantic route to Latin America uneconomic and abandoned it in 1964 to British United Airways (BUA), an independent airline. In October 1970 BUA merged with Caledonian Airways, the independent Scottish charter airline, and it is to be assumed that the new, enlarged company will continue to operate its South American flights.

BOAC recommenced the direct flights to Singapore and Australia in January-April 1946 and to the United States in July 1946. No souvenir covers were carried on these first flights, however, and it was not until the inauguration of the route to Japan in March 1948 that such souvenirs were provided. In December 1949 the first Stratocruiser flight from London to New York took place. In May 1952 BOAC inaugurated the world's first jet airline, with flights by Comet-1 linking London and Johannesburg. Appropriately BOAC took due note of the importance of this occasion to produce its own souvenir covers. Later the same year souvenir covers were used for the first flights of Comet-1 to Colombo (August) and Singapore (October).

The next major development was the introduction of the prop-jet airliner, Bristol Britannias being used on all major services from 1957 onwards. In October 1958 the Comet-4 airliner was brought into service on the London-New York route and was gradually adopted for other important routes. All of these first flights were signalised by souvenir covers. In March-April 1959 BOAC established its first round-world service, using Britannia aircraft from London to Tokyo (via New York and San Francisco) and Comet-4 jets for the section from Tokyo to London. It is a matter of some regret, however, that this momentous occasion was allowed to pass without aerophilatelic commemoration. The same has been true of many of the important landmarks in the Corporation's development since that date, as, for example, when VC-10 airliners were introduced on various routes in the 1960s.

Pan-American Airways

In the 1920s the United States instituted a system of Foreign Air Mail (FAM) services to South and Central America, Canada and the West Indies. The first of these FAMs came into operation on 1 October 1928 between New York and Montreal. In many cases these routes were already in existence but were re-designated from 1928 onwards with FAM numbers.

In 1929 two companies, Pan-American Airways and NYRBA, began operating airmail flights in the West Indies and Latin America respectively under United States postal contract. In 1930 NYRBA was merged with Pan-American Airways and in

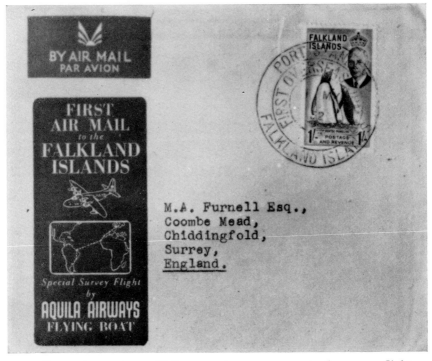

38 The Air Gram produced by Siam (Thailand) in 1933. The Siamese Air Gram was a forerunner of the air letter sheet (aerogramme) introduced in the Second World War

39 Souvenir envelope of May 1952 to commemorate the survey flight from the Falkland Islands to England by Aquila Airways

40 Triptych on cover carried by the Balbo squadron on its mass formation flight from Italy to the United States and back in 1933

the ensuing decade Pan-Am gradually developed its aerial routes on both the Atlantic and Pacific routes. In May 1937 Pan-Am inaugurated its trans-Atlantic service with trial flights between Bermuda and New York. The following month the first commercial flight on this run was made by the Pan-American flying boat *Bermuda Clipper*. Survey flights across the Atlantic between Botwood (Newfoundland) and Foynes (Ireland) were made in July/August 1937 by *Clipper III* eventually linking New York, Bermuda, the Azores, Newfoundland and Iceland. On all of these flights special covers and pictorial cachets were provided.

In November 1937 the Pan-Am flying boat base was altered to Baltimore and from there flights were made across the Atlantic via Bermuda. In March 1938 this route was officially designated FAM 17, mail being flown in either direction by either Pan-Am or Imperial Airways. In 1939 the trans-Atlantic route was changed during the winter months to Baltimore-Southampton via the Azores, Lisbon, Bordeaux and Marseilles. The Pan-Am flights over this Southern Route were formally inaugurated in May 1939. Special cachets were applied to mail taken aboard at the various points en route. The Northern Route, from New York to Southampton via Shediac, Botwood and Foynes came into operation in June 1939. Special covers and cachets were used on both outward and inward journeys. During the Second World War Pan-Am operated flights from Lisbon to New York. In December 1941 Pan-Am's *Cape Town Clipper* established a South Atlantic route from Miami to Leopoldville via San Juan, Port of Spain, Belem, Natal, Bathurst and Lagos and this route was later extended to cover the Gold Coast and Liberia.

In the Pacific area Pan-American Airways instituted trans-Pacific flights in November 1935 when the flying boat *China Clipper* flew to the Philippine Islands from San Francisco via Hawaii and Guam. Special 25c airmail stamps, showing the *China Clipper*, were released in time for the inaugural flight. Similar stamps, without the commemorative date, and in denominations of 20c and 50c, were introduced two years later for the Pan-Am flights from San Francisco to China. This service was terminated as a result of the Pacific campaign in the Second World War when the Japanese overran much of the northern Pacific and China. In May 1941 Pan-Am extended their trans-Pacific service to Hong Kong and Singapore, using either place as alternative termini. In the postwar period Pan-Am began operating mail flights between Singapore and Saigon in May 1953 and in the 1950s extended operations to cover the major cities of Europe and Asia. In 1959 a Boeing 707 of Pan-Am made a non-stop flight from Seattle to Rome, a distance of 5,830 miles. A special cachet inscribed FIRST JET NON-STOP POLAR FLIGHT was applied to souvenir mail. Pan-Am inaugurated a round-the-world jet freighter service on 1 July 1965 and a pictorial cachet showing a map of the route was struck on 'first flight' covers. Pan-Am now heads the list of the world's airlines, both in the mileage covered by its routes and in the amount of freight, mail and passengers flown.

10

The Last of the Pioneer Flights

By 1930 commercial aviation had become firmly established in all but the most backward countries and the major air routes of the world had been explored, if not yet fully developed. It would seem, therefore, that there was little scope left to aviators of adventurous spirit and yet the decade immediately before the Second World War witnessed quite a number of epic flights, by solo fliers at one extreme and by mass squadrons at the other. Flying still retained something of the glamour and novelty which had surrounded it in the early days and the famous aviators of this decade, such as James Mollison and Amy Johnson, Amelia Earhart, Jean Mermoz, Wiley Post and Maryse Bastie, captured the imagination of countless millions throughout the world. These fliers, and many others, left their mark on aerophilately, with flown covers and souvenir cachets. Some of them had stamps issued in their honour, either in their lifetime or in later commemoration of their deeds.

While the Germans were gaining a virtual monopoly of the Atlantic service, by means of their airship *Graf Zeppelin*, the French were attempting to bridge the South Atlantic by heavier-than-air machines. The prime mover in this scheme was the aviator, Jean Mermoz who, with Dabry and Gimie, formed the French Compagnie Generale Aeropostale. The inaugural flight of this company across the South Atlantic took place in May 1930. Mail was despatched by aircraft from Toulouse on 11 May and Mermoz flew via St Louis to the South Atlantic island of Fernando da Noronha and thence to Natal in Brazil. The mail was off-loaded at Natal on 13 May. Mermoz and his two companions attempted a return flight on 8 July but were forced down in the Atlantic about 500 miles west of St Louis and were rescued by the steamship *Phocee*. The mailbags were salvaged and the letters subsequently backstamped in Paris on

16 July. A second experimental flight by the Compagnie General Aeropostale was made between France and Brazil, via Morocco in January 1933. Mermoz and five others left France on 12 January and reached Rio de Janeiro the following day. They flew on to Buenos Aires, arriving in that city on 22 January. Between 15 and 21 May Mermoz flew from Natal via Dakar to Paris, carrying airmail from South America. A year later Mermoz undertook a mail flight on the same route, on behalf of Air France. Mail reached Chile 77 hours after leaving Paris. At the end of July Mermoz and Gimie flew from Natal via the Cape Verde Islands to Villa Cisneros in Spanish North Africa on an experimental flight on behalf of Air France. Mermoz and his colleagues, Bonnot, Hebrard, Gautier and Gimie, made several other flights across the South Atlantic that year.

During 1935 and 1936 Mermoz made numerous flights across the South Atlantic and in August 1936 France paid tribute to the work of her airmen in this field by issuing a pair of stamps commemorating the hundredth crossing by planes of the Compagnie Generale Aeropostale or Air France. Then, on 7 December the seaplane *Croix du Sud*, with the aviators Mermoz, Pichodon, Ezan, Cruvelher and Lavidalic on board, was lost at sea. Two stamps portraying Jean Mermoz were released the following April in his memory.

Perhaps the best-known British aviators in the thirties were the Mollisons. Amy Johnson had already established a reputation as an intrepid solo flier, with a long distance flight to Cape Town, before she met James Mollison. Mollison, an ex-RAF pilot who had turned to civil aviation in Australia, broke off his honeymoon in August 1932 to prepare for the first solo, nonstop flight across the Atlantic from east to west. At 11.30 a.m. on 18 August he took off in a D.H. Puss Moth *Heart's Content*, from Portmarnock, Ireland, and flew for 30 hours 15 minutes to land in New Brunswick, Canada. Two days later he flew on to Roosevelt Field, New York, and a tumultuous welcome. On his arrival Mollison was presented with the gold medal of the City of New York and, in turn, he handed over an official letter of greeting from the Lord Mayor of Dublin to the Mayor of New York. The cover which contained this historic letter bore the Gold Seal of Dublin, the Red Seal of St John's, New Brunswick, and the Civic Seal of New York, with various endorsements and autographs. Several other covers with similar embellishments were also flown. A few of the contemporary Irish shilling stamps were unofficially overprinted ATLANTIC AIR MAIL 1932 in three lines. Several covers are known bearing this stamp and a block of four unused examples is in the Fitzgerald Collection. On 28 August Mollison attempted a flight from New York to England, but the flight was abandoned at Halifax, Nova Scotia, on account of Mollison's illness.

In February 1933 Mollison flew from Lympne in England via Villa Cisneros, Natal and Rio de Janeiro to Buenos Aires. A few covers are known with the Lympne Air Port Despatch cachet of 6 February and the Natal postmark of 9 February. Although the Mollisons made a number of world flights, they had perhaps the dubious record of the most crashes of any of the epic aviators of the period. On 8 June 1933, while setting out on a flight from Croydon to the United States their machine crashed on take-off and was badly damaged. On 22 July the Mollisons had a second go, taking off this time from Pendine Sands in Wales. They arrived at Bridgewater in the United States the following day but crashed their *Seafarer* on landing. Neither of them was seriously hurt and the small quantity of souvenir covers which they carried were undamaged. On 3 October they set off from Wasaga Beach for the return flight to Europe. Their aircraft was damaged in taking off and the flight subsequently abandoned. The Mollisons later made a number of flights across the Atlantic and to Australia, some successful, some abortive. Their marriage was as tempestuous as their flying and eventually they separated. Mollison gave up long-distance flying at the end of the thirties but gained the MBE as a wartime ferry pilot. Mrs Mollison also became a wartime ferry pilot for the RAF and lost her life when her aircraft crashed in the Thames Estuary in 1941.

If anything the thirties was a decade of the lady pilot. Having achieved social and political emancipation in the twenties there seemed nothing that a woman could not do as well, if not better, than a man, and in pioneer aviation women felt that there was yet time for them to make their mark before the men could monopolise it. As early as 1918 there had been Katherine Stinson and Ruth Law, making a name for themselves by their flights in Canada and the Philippines respectively, but nevertheless flying continued to be a predominantly male profession till the 1930s. In 1931 Mrs Beryl Hart made an attempted flight from New York to Paris with Lieut W. S.

MacLaren. Their plane was lost at sea after leaving Bermuda, though mail flown from New York to Bermuda is recorded. The following year Ruth R. Nichols made an unsuccessful attempt on the New York-Paris flight, crashing near St John's, New Brunswick. Covers carried on this flight bore the cachet FIRST WOMAN'S SOLO TRANS-ATLANTIC ATTEMPT, NEW YORK TO PARIS, LOCKHEED VEGA MONOPLANE AKITA N R 496M, RUTH R. NICHOLS, with the additional endorsement PLANE CRASHED AT ST JOHN'S NEW BRUNSWICK, JUNE 22 1931. In September 1932 Miss Edna Newcomer, with two men, W. Ulbrich and Dr Leon M. Pisculli, attempted to fly from New York to Rome but were lost at sea. Several flights were made in the thirties by Colonel Charles Lindbergh and his wife, the most notable being from the United States to Denmark, via Labrador, Greenland, and Shetland, in July-August 1933 and from Bathurst, Gambia, to Natal in Brazil in December of the same year. Souvenir postcards and a few covers are known from these flights. In November 1935 Miss Jean Batten flew from London to Buenos Aires via Dakar and Natal and, again, some souvenir mail was carried.

In September 1936 Mrs Beryl Markham became the first woman to fly the Atlantic from east to west. She took off from Abingdon, Berkshire, on 4 September and landed the following day at Baleine Cove, Nova Scotia. Some 26 covers, signed by Mrs Markham, were flown. A cachet giving details of the flight was applied to the covers on their arrival in Canada. On 30 December 1936 the Frenchwoman, Maryse Bastie, flew from Dakar to Natal in a record time of 12 hours 5 minutes for the South Atlantic crossing, during her flight from Paris to Buenos Aires. In 1955 France issued a 50fr airmail stamp bearing her portrait and depicting the monoplane in which she made her record flight.

Unquestionably the most celebrated of all women aviators was Amelia Earhart (Mrs Putnam). In June 1928 she became the first woman to cross the Atlantic by air, flying as a passenger with W. Stultz and Louis Gordon from Newfoundland to South Wales in a Fokker seaplane *Friendship*. On that occasion three covers were carried, postmarked at Trepassey, Newfoundland, on 16 June and backstamped in London on 21 June. Almost four years later, however, she piloted her own plane from Newfoundland to Ireland to become the first woman to make an Atlantic solo flight. Fifty covers, franked with American 5c stamps postmarked at New York on 13 May 1932 were backstamped at Londonderry on 23 May and marked with a souvenir cachet. In April 1935 she made a goodwill flight from the United States to Mexico and the latter country issued an airmail stamp with a commemorative overprint to mark the occasion. In 1937 Miss Earhart set out with Captain Fred Noonan on an attempted world flight. They flew from the United States across the Caribbean to Dutch Guiana (Surinam). In June 1967 Surinam released two stamps portraying Miss Earhart to commemorate the thirtieth anniversary of this flight. From Surinam she flew to Natal and thence across the Atlantic to St Louis, setting up a new record for the west-east crossing of 13 hours 22 minutes. The flight proceeded satisfactorily until Miss Earhart was on the cross-Pacific stage. Rumour has it that, acting on secret instructions from the United States government, she took a detour over the Japanese occupied Caroline Islands to carry out some clandestine aerial reconnaissance, and that she was intercepted by Japanese fighters and forced down. Whether she died in captivity or actually crashed into the Pacific without trace is not known. The souvenir mail which was to have been carried round the world and postmarked at the various stopping places en route, was lost with her. The United States issued an airmail stamp in 1963 depicting Amelia Earhart and her ill-fated Lockheed Electra.

Italian Mass Flights

Mention has already been made, in Chapter 6, of Gabriele D'Annunzio and his plans for mass flights to the Far East. D'Annunzio's ideas inspired his disciple, General Italo Balbo, to organise similar flights in the thirties. Balbo, one of the most colourful figures in aviation between the wars, first came to prominence in October 1922 as commander of the Fascist *squadre* (storm-troops) which led the famous march on Rome which brought Mussolini to power. Balbo later became Minister of Aviation in the Fascist government and set out to build up the *Regia Aeronautica*, just as Göring in Germany later developed the *Luftwaffe*, into one of the world's most formidable air forces.

Balbo's first essay in international mass flights came in December 1930 when he commanded a squadron of 12 flying boats on a flight from Rome to Rio de Janeiro. Eleven of the machines successfully completed the flight, arriving in Rio on

15 January. A special 7.70 lire air stamp was issued by Italy to mark the occasion. The design symbolised the mass flight of Savoia-Marchetti flying boats, with the Southern Cross constellation featured in the background. A special airmail postmark inscribed CROCIERA ITALIA BRASILE (Crossing Italy-Brazil) was used to cancel these stamps on flown covers. This stamp was issued privately in December 1930 and not released to the general public until 27 January 1931.

In July 1933 Balbo commanded a flight of 24 flying boats on a mission from Italy to the United States in connection with the Century of Progress World's Fair at Chicago. The Balbo squadron left Orbetello on 5 July and flew via Amsterdam, Londonderry, Iceland, Labrador, Shediac and Montreal to Chicago where they landed on 15 July. Mail from Italy, Holland, Iceland, Shediac and Montreal was carried by these aircraft to Chicago. A special airmail label was produced by Iceland while a commemorative vignette was issued by Italy. But the most fantastic issue of air stamps ever made also appeared in connection with this flight. Basically it consisted of two triptychs, the left-hand portion of each consisting of an undenominated registration stamp featuring the Italian tricolour, the central portion (portraying King Victor Emmanuel III) prepaying the ordinary postage, and the right-hand portion prepaying the postage as far as Iceland (19.75 lire) or the United States (44.75 lire). The left-hand and central portions of both triptychs were similar in design and value but the right-hand portion featured a figure of Flight in a four-horse chariot following in the wake of the squadron (19.75 lire) and the flight of the aircraft over the northern hemisphere, with the Coliseum in Rome and the Chicago skyline on either side (44.75 lire). Each value was issued in 20 strips of three, differing in the registration stamps which were overprinted with the abbreviated names of 20 pilots.

In connection with official correspondence sent via the armada to New York, the higher denomination was produced in different colours overprinted SERVIZIO DI STATO. Covers bearing this State Service triptych were addressed to President Roosevelt, the Mayors of New York and Chicago and various other dignitaries. Only 80 of these triptychs are said to have been printed. The higher denomination was also overprinted VOLO DI RITORNO (Return Flight) but was never put into use. The mail which left Rome consisted of 136 mailbags (approximately 19,000 pieces). About 8,400 items were destined for

European stops, Amsterdam, Londonderry and Reykjavik. A special cancellation CROCIERA AEREA DEL DECENNALE—ITALIA—NORD AMERICA was applied to this souvenir mail.

Iceland overprinted three of her contemporary definitive stamps with a diagonal inscription HOPFLUG ITALA 1933 and these stamps were used to frank correspondence flown by the Balbo squadron to the United States. Some 298 covers were carried on this flight. On the return flight from Chicago to Rome in August 1933 mail was flown from the United States, Canada and Newfoundland. For this occasion Newfoundland overprinted the 75c airmail stamp 1933 GEN BALBO FLIGHT and surcharged it with the new value $4.50 to prepay the special air fee. This overprint was applied in a setting of eight and eight stamps are known to have been overprinted upside down. Four of these were kept intact in a block but the others were cut to pieces. Subsequently the four mutilated copies were reconstructed and despite the fact that they are damaged they now fetch high prices. The block of four was sold for £20,000 at the sale of the Vivian Hewitt Collection by Robson Lowe in 1969 and was later split into singles by the purchaser, Mr M. A. Bojanowicz, for resale to other collectors. Eight examples are known in which this overprint was applied to the 10c airmail stamp by mistake. A mint copy of this error is preserved in the Fitzgerald Collection. On his return to Italy Balbo was promoted to the rank of Marshal, but resigned from the Air Ministry in November 1933 as a result of disagreements with his colleagues. During the Second World War he returned to combat duties but died in mysterious circumstances (some say on the orders of Mussolini) in 1942.

Other World Flights

At the height of the Depression of 1931 American morale received a much-needed boost from the flight round the world by a one-eyed ex-parachutist Wiley Post and Harold Gatty in their Lockheed Vega *Winnie Mae*. Their time for the round-world flight was 8 days, 15 hours and 51 minutes. Souvenir mail was carried by the aviators and posted at various stages en route. Two years later, in July 1933, Wiley Post flew round the world alone in *Winnie Mae* and furnished the world with the most remarkable example of flying endurance up to that time. The Sperry Gyroscope Company had perfected an automatic pilot device the previous year and with the aid of this device and a radio direction finder, Post was able to cut down the number of stops required on the global flight. In this way he succeeded in slashing his previous time by almost a day—7 days, 18 hours and 50 minutes. A few souvenir covers were carried on this flight. Wiley Post was killed two years later in an air crash near Point Barrow, Alaska.

Shortly after Post's death an American millionaire, Howard Hughes, established a new world speed record of 325 m.p.h. with his aircraft *Hughes Special*. In July 1938 Hughes and four companions flew a Lockheed 14 round the world in the fantastic time of 3 days, 19 hours and 14 minutes. Again a small souvenir mail was carried on this trip, and postmarked at various points en route. Although Hughes had financed the flight and equipped the aircraft with all the latest devices his modesty was characteristic. 'Please remember,' he said after the flight,

'that I am but one of the five persons who made that trip, and being taller than any of them kept getting in the way and making a nuisance of myself. If you must praise anyone, save your shouts for Wiley Post, for by flying around the world alone, in the time he did, and with but one eye, he made the most amazing flight that has ever occurred.'

11

The Second World War and
its Repercussions

By the time of the outbreak of the Second World War in
September 1939 aviation, in both its civil and military applications, had been highly developed. As was the case in the First
World War, this was a period which witnessed tremendous
progress in aeronautics. Aeroplanes developed in size, range
and speed beyond anything dreamed of in the prewar years,
the jet age dawned with the development, in Britain and
Germany, of jet-propelled aircraft as early as 1941 and their
practical application to fighter planes before the war in Europe
had ended. The development of pilotless planes and later
rockets, capable of delivering an explosive warhead over several
hundreds of miles to the target, foreshadowed the space race of
the 1950s and 1960s and the interplanetary travel whose
threshold man has now crossed.

Aircraft were used with greater impact than could have been
imagined even in 1939. It was carrier-based aircraft, raiding
Pearl Harbour, which brought the United States into the war,
and it was an aircraft, the *Enola Gay*, which put Japan out of
the war by dropping the first atomic bomb in 1945. Airborne
troops in the Low Countries in 1940, in Crete in 1941 and in
Normandy in 1944, changed the course of whole campaigns and
the great naval battles of the Pacific theatre of operations were
largely fought by carrier-based aircraft. The Battle of Britain
was an aerial one and it was by means of ever larger and more
sophisticated bombers that total war came to have such a grim
meaning for the civilian populations of countries far removed
from the front line.

It was axiomatic, therefore, that the war should play an
enormous part in the development of airmail. While the
majority of the great air routes pioneered in the immediate prewar years had to be closed for the duration of hostilities, the

carriage of mail for military personnel increased tremendously and significantly established the view that first class mail should be transmitted by air whenever possible. Before the war the carriage of letters by aircraft was still regarded as something of a luxury. As a result of the war, however, people began to take the carriage of mail by air for granted, and the differential between air and surface methods of mail transportation after the war made the former all the more advantageous. Since the bulk of mail during the war was eventually carried by air there was never the same desire to distinguish it from surface mail and thus there were not the cachets and endorsements which denoted the emergency airmails of the First World War. Aerophilatelists have had to console themselves by collecting examples of covers bearing RAF Post Office and censor markings, or the rare German 'Inselpost' mail carried by air to and from the beleaguered islands of the Aegean towards the end of the war. Nevertheless the Second World War produced a vast amount of material of interest to the airmail collector. The use of propaganda leaflets was greatly accelerated, while two important methods of speeding up mail and saving aircraft space were devised. In both of these cases, however, the idea had existed before the war but the war itself had greatly stimulated interest and encouraged the development of these methods.

Aerogrammes

Most books on philately give Britain the credit for pioneering the air letter sheet or aerogramme, with the introduction early in 1941 of special forms printed on thin paper and intended for the use of military forces serving overseas. These air letter sheets took up very little space compared with ordinary letters and were so successful that in August of the same year their use was extended to civilians. Special sheets inscribed PRISONERS OF WAR AIR MAIL in English and German or Japanese were employed on communications permitted through the International Red Cross. These sheets had a $2\frac{1}{2}$d stamp imprinted on them. The Forces Air Letter sheets bore 3d stamps while those used by civilians bore 6d stamps. It is interesting to note that, while other postal rates increased in the postwar years, the air letter rate remained stationary at 6d until 1966.

Although Britain's air letter sheets inspired several other

countries to imitate them during the war, while many others adopted them afterwards, it is not generally known that this expedient, or something like it, had existed for several years before the war. As long ago as 1933 special stationery known as Air Mail Letter Cards had been used in Iraq and Palestine. These items consisted of thin sheets of paper, with imprinted stamps and airmail labels. The sender folded the sheet to conform in size and shape with a blue border printed on the address side of the sheet, and gummed flaps were provided for sealing the sheet. This device was invented by an Englishman, Douglas Gumbley, who served as Director of Posts to the Iraqi Government in the early 1930s. He designed the Air Mail Letter Card, realising the need for a lightweight form of specific size which could be carried easily by the newly developed air services in the Middle East. Normal letters, carried overland, being of varying weight and size, seemed likely to be much too expensive and impractical for air transportation. Mr Gumbley designed an Air Letter card and registered it at Stationer's Hall in February 1933 under his own copyright. The first of these air letters was used in Iraq and subsequently their use was extended to Palestine, then under British mandate, where Mr Gumbley was in charge of postal matters in the latter part of the 1930s. Australian forces were stationed in Palestine at the beginning of the war and their authorities arranged with Mr Gumbley that special forces air letters should be made available, at the rate of one per man each week. There is some evidence to suggest that it was the initiative of the Australians which led the British military forces to adopt air letters; on the other hand it is not unlikely that the British authorities arrived at the same idea independently.

After the Second World War these handy, lightweight sheets spread rapidly to many other countries and nowadays their use is almost universal, though, curiously, France has only now adopted them. The majority of air letter sheets have a stamp printed on them, although some countries, such as New Zealand, Ireland and Rhodesia, issue them unstamped and adhesives have to be affixed. In recent years these sheets have been used effectively for tourist publicity. In Britain pictorial aerogrammes made their debut in 1965 when two sheets, featuring the Tower of London and the Houses of Parliament, were released. This experiment was apparently unsuccessful since it was never extended or repeated. Nevertheless many countries have made good use of the pictorial aerogrammes to boost tourism.

One of the first countries to introduce aerogrammes of this sort was Rhodesia which, in the 1950s, issued them with rather crudely typographed blocks in the lower left-hand corner, extolling the beauties of the nature reserves and the scenery of the country. In more recent years Rhodesia has issued aerogrammes with pictures in full colour. Many British Commonwealth countries have produced colourful tourist aerogrammes in recent years. Britain, Australia and New Zealand are among those which annually issue special Christmas greetings aerogrammes. During the period following the Unilateral Declaration of Independence Rhodesia produced several aerogrammes containing printed messages aimed at friends and relations of Rhodesians overseas. These propaganda air letters are the latest development in what has come to be known as psychological warfare.

The term 'aerogramme' was officially adopted at the 13th Universal Postal Union Congress held in Brussels in 1951-2 and this is found inscribed on these sheets, although Britain persists in using the term 'Air Letter' in addition. The collecting and study of aerogrammes is now a major branch of aerophilately, with catalogues, handbooks and periodical literature devoted solely to it.

Airgraphs

Contemporary with the air letter sheet was the airgraph, an ingenious device born of necessity in 1941 when air communication between Britain and the Middle East was circuitous as a result of Italian military action in the Mediterranean and North African regions. As even surface mail became precarious, on account of the dangers to shipping presented by submarines and aerial bombardment, the British government resurrected a project which had been put before them in 1932 by the Kodak photographic company. Kodak had invented a camera which reproduced on film documents of the dimensions of bank cheques. It had been suggested that this apparatus could be used to reduce the bulk and weight of airmail correspondence, if the public could be persuaded to write their messages on special forms which would then be reduced photographically, flown to their destination, and then enlarged and reproduced in readable size for delivery to the addressee. The General Post

Office rejected this scheme at the time since it was felt that the public would never agree to the use of form-filling or consent to their messages being exposed for all to see.

The exigencies of war, however, induced the authorities to reconsider this project, for the use of personnel stationed in the Middle East. Kodak supplied equipment and technicians who were flown out to Cairo to set up a processing station. A standard form was designed and a charge of 3d per airgraph was sanctioned. The first form had an address panel at the foot but subsequent printings had the panel at the top. Space was provided for the message to be written, in bold, legible handwriting. Completed forms were reduced to microfilm and countless thousands were flown back to England where they were processed at Kodak's Wealdstone plant near London. Within 24 hours the prints were passed on to London Postal Region. They were folded, placed in window envelopes and despatched to the recipients. The envelopes bore the word 'Airgraph' printed in blue on buff paper.

The first airgraphs from the Middle East reached England on 13 May, having left Cairo on 21 April 1941. In August 1941 an airgraph service in the opposite direction was instituted. Airgraph message forms were made available in all post offices. Completed forms were sent to London Postal Region who forwarded them to Kodak for photography. Eventually Kodak had accommodation in the Foreign Section of the General Post Office for processing airgraphs. Each airgraph was given a serial number in the top right-hand corner and arranged in bundles of 1,700—the number which could be photographed on one 100-foot length of film. A complete film weighed only $5\frac{1}{2}$ ounces. After photography the original airgraph forms were retained until it was confirmed that the film had reached its destination safely. When a film was lost or damaged the required airgraphs could be identified by their serial numbers and re-photographed. In September 1942 the flying boat *Clare*, carrying some 55,000 airgraphs on film, was lost and the originals had to be re-processed. The second batch of airgraphs was delivered within a fortnight of the loss of the *Clare*.

Following the initial success of the airgraph scheme other processing stations were established at Nairobi, Johannesburg, Bombay, Melbourne, Wellington and Toronto, followed, as the war progressed, by stations at Algiers, Naples, Calcutta and Colombo. Quite a collection can be made of the different types of airgraphs, forms and envelopes used all over the British Commonwealth by the end of the war. In addition special printed airgraph greetings forms were issued by Britain, India, New Zealand and South Africa, by the Polish Army Corps, the RAF and military formations down to regimental or squadron level. Towards the end of the war the General Post Office introduced an airmail rate of $1\frac{1}{2}$d for a one-ounce letter from Britain to forces serving abroad and permitted letters from troops on active service to be sent home by air free of postage. This scheme, introduced in February 1945, 'underpriced' the airgraphs. As the necessity for them vanished with the return to more normal conditions the airgraph was doomed. The airgraph had been declining in popularity since the 6d civilian air letter had been introduced in 1944. On 31 July 1945 the Post Office closed down its airgraph scheme. In four years some 350 million airgraphs had been transmitted. The total weight of the film involved had been no more than 50 tons—compared with the minimum of 4,500 tons which a comparable number of ordinary letters would have weighed.

Propaganda Leaflets

As has been mentioned in Chapter 1, one of the earliest motives for transmitting messages by air was propaganda in times of war. This weapon was used to some extent in the First World War, but was developed to a fine art during the Second World War, all the belligerents making use of leaflets not only directed against each other but also at neutral countries whom they hoped to influence. Some idea of the scope of operations involved may be gained from the fact that 2,088 different types of leaflet were disseminated from British bases alone. In August 1943 aeroplanes operating from Britain dropped over 70 million leaflets on European territory. The leaflets dropped by British and American aircraft may be divided into three classes: those dropped over their own territory (Wings for Victory, Salute the Soldier Week and similar publicity leaflets in connection with patriotic fund-raising projects), those dropped on enemy territory or aimed primarily at enemy troops, and those dropped over enemy occupied territory, aimed at the civilian population. Leaflets aimed at the enemy troops often featured cosy domestic scenes or lovely girls, reminding the luckless soldiers in the trenches, facing death and disease, of happier days before the

41 First Flight cover marking the introduction of the Loftleidir North Atlantic service by Rolls-Royce 400 Jet Prop aircraft, 1964. Postmarked at Jamaica, New York (Kennedy International Airport) and back-stamped on arrival in Luxembourg, for onward transmission to England

42 Aerogramme from Kennedy Airport to London, with the cachet celebrating the 25th anniversary of Pan AM's North Atlantic mail service, 1964

43 An early example of a letter carried by rocket. Note the special stamp and postal markings used on mail carried in the trial firing between Scarp and Harris in the Outer Hebrides, July 1934

44 The envelope carried to the moon by the Apollo 12 astronauts, franked by a proof of the 'moon' stamp and bearing a special moon landing cancellation

war. Leaflets aimed at civilians in enemy-occupied territory gave war news, raised morale with promises that the 'second front' was imminent, or in more positive terms gave advice or orders to the various resistance movements.

The Germans dropped leaflets on Britain or on Allied troops in the combat zones, their theme being to undermine Allied morale or to divide Briton from Frenchman or turn Briton against American. The Germans were also adept at forging the leaflets dropped by the British and Americans to the French Resistance fighters, giving false information or instructions. The Allies, in turn, dropped leaflets exposing these frauds.

The material dropped over enemy-occupied territory constitutes the most interesting type of all. British aircraft dropped packets of 20 cigarettes over Holland to celebrate the birthday of Queen Wilhelmina, and subsequently these changed hands on the Dutch black market for as much as £3 a packet. In 1943 the United States Army Air Force dropped leaflets over Warsaw wrapped round little sachets of instant coffee. The leaflets, which were gummed on the back, consisted of 'Wanted' posters for Hans Frank, Minister of the Interior in the Nazi Generalgouvernment of wartime Poland. The idea was that finders of these leaflets would stick them on the walls of buildings and keep the coffee as a reward. The text of the leaflet recited the war crimes of Hans Frank and promised retribution at the end of the war.

The Allies also dropped leaflets over Italy and Japan, in the former case to undermine Italian morale and in the latter to spread panic and confusion. The Japanese superstition that disaster will occur if the kiri leaf falls before its time was cunningly exploited by the Americans who dropped thousands of leaflets, shaped and coloured like kiri leaves, out of season. Both the Germans and the Allies dropped what appeared on first glance to be banknotes but which turned out, on closer inspection, to be forgeries containing propaganda messages. Britain forged German stamps for use on postcards purporting to contain war news or reproducing German anti-Nazi messages. The Germans retaliated in kind, dropping leaflets from aircraft disguised with pseudo-Allied markings over France, Belgium and Denmark. The messages were calculated to turn the civilian population against their impending liberation. Leaflets dropped on Denmark, for example, promised that Russian troops were coming to liberate them, others that Negro troops would be used in the liberation, and so on. When Allied bombing directed against military targets in Belgium unfortunately hit civilians, the Germans followed the raid with leaflets inscribed 'Yesterday we threw down leaflets to encourage you; today we threw down bombs to liberate you. One cannot make omelettes without breaking eggs, so if you are an egg, God save the king!' In addition the Germans imposed severe penalties on anyone found in possession of Allied leaflets.

In the autumn of 1944 some British prisoners of war in German hospitals were given an extra letter form on which to write home to their families for Christmas. Leaflets were printed with these messages reproduced, and an inscription asking the finder to forward the message to the addressee. German agents in Britain were on the look out for these messages and were supposed to observe the postmarks on these missives coming through the post. The messages themselves were despatched in the earliest V1 rocket planes, being released immediately before the rocket plummeted to earth. In this way the Germans hoped to gather information about the exact location of the point of impact of these rockets. Fortunately the majority of leaflets disseminated in this way were recovered by the authorities and it is unlikely that German Intelligence gleaned much data from this exercise.

Aerial propaganda leaflets have been a feature of every military campaign since the end of the Second World War. They were used by the British in Cyprus, Malaya, Kenya and during the Indonesian confrontation in North Borneo. In the Korean War and, more recently, in Vietnam, leaflets were dropped by the belligerents on each others troops as well as on the civilian populace caught up in both conflicts. Propaganda leaflets also have their peaceful uses, being employed in publicity stunts and goodwill flights. Leaflets packed in PVC with small cork floats were dropped by aircraft of Coastal Command in 1954 over the Atlantic west of the British Isles. These packets floated on the Atlantic currents and most of them were eventually washed up on beaches extending from Iceland to Ireland, from Shetland to the Scillies, and even along the Continental coastline from Arctic Russia to Portugal. The finders of these packets were asked to complete a form inside, giving the position of the find and the name and address of the finder. A reward of 2s 6d was sent to the finders by the National Institute of Oceanography in England which used these drift-cards to plot ocean currents and thus determine the likelihood of beaches becoming polluted by ships discharging oil at sea.

12

Airmails by Other Methods

Pigeon Posts

Mention has already been made, in Chapter 1, of the earliest
form of airmail known to man—the carrier pigeon. It is not
generally known that at least one other kind of bird has been
recorded as used for this purpose. In the middle of the nineteenth century tame frigate-birds were used in the Ellice Islands
of the South Pacific in much the same way as carrier pigeons.
The natives were encouraged to take the young birds without
injuring or frightening them. Comfortable sheltered perches
were erected near the beach, the young birds were tied to these
by the leg, and fed until they were tame. When they were then
let loose, the birds would go to sea for food and return to their
perches when fed and satisfied with flying. The Christian
missionaries in the islands observed the regular homing habits
of these birds and thus devised the frigate-bird post. They sent
and received letters rolled up tightly and inserted in a quill
which was attached to the bird. Very little is known regarding
the operation of this service. It is perhaps fitting that the frigate-
bird was depicted on the stamps of the Gilbert and Ellice Islands
when their first pictorial series was introduced in 1939.

Although the Ellice Islands bird mail has left no mark in the
stamp album, farther south there existed one of the most famous
pigeon postal services of all time, which has resulted in
numerous items of interest to the aerophilatelist. During 1896
Mr W. Fricker made several successful experimental flights
with pigeons between the Great Barrier Islands and the city of
Auckland in the north island of New Zealand. As a result of
these experiments he inaugurated, early in 1897, a regular
pigeon post between the Great Barrier Island and Okupu,
where Miss Springall doubled as postmistress and agent for the

pigeon service. A few months later Mr Fricker transferred his headquarters to Oroville, some four miles inland from Okupu, where Dr D. McMillan conducted the agency.

In May 1897 Mr J. E. Parkin resurrected the original Okupu agency but abandoned it a year later, passing it eventually to Mr S. Holden Howie of Auckland who took over the service. Later he extended it to include Port Fitzroy on Great Barrier Island, Whangaparapara, Port Charles, Waikeke Island, Marotiri and to an ostrich farm at Whitford Park. On the suggestion of Mr H. Bolitho adhesive stamps were introduced for use in connection with this service on 19 November 1898. These stamps were printed by the Observer Printing Works, Auckland and were the first distinctive adhesive stamps for use on correspondence ever to be carried by air (if we discount the labels of the Buffalo Balloon Post of 1877). Altogether eight different stamps were produced by the two rival organisations which operated pigeon posts in this area. The pigeon posts were of great benefit to the residents of the islands in the Hauraki Gulf, and of commercial value to the mining community on Great Barrier Island. The services operated respectively by Fricker and Howie came to an end on 26 September 1908 when the Government telegraph service was extended from Port Charles on the mainland to Tryphena on Great Barrier Island.

The first issue of stamps made by the Original Great Barrier Pigeongram Service (as the company operated by Howie and Bolitho was known) consisted of 1s blue stamps. The simple motif showed a pigeon in flight with a letter in its beak. The stamps were inscribed GREAT BARRIER ISLAND SPECIAL POST with the value, in words, expressed in the vertical sides. Between March and June 1899 a modified form of this design, with the frame more ornately embellished, was used for 1s stamps printed in greenish-blue. The New Zealand postal authorities objected to the inscription SPECIAL POST and to counteract this the organisers had to overprint the stamps PIGEONGRAM. Only some 960 stamps were thus overprinted and very few of these appear to have been used. In July the design of the stamps was redrawn with the word PIGEONGRAM in place of the offending inscription. In August 1899 unused stocks of the stamp inscribed SPECIAL POST were overprinted MAROTIRI PIGEONGRAM in two lines for use on the service operating between Auckland and Marotiri on the Hen and Chicken Islands (about 30 miles north-west of the Great Barrier Island) where the Copper Mines Syndicate was working. An entirely new design in red was produced for shilling stamps used by the Syndicate in September 1899. Inscribed MAROTIRI ISLAND PIGEON GRAM in a circle with a pigeon in the centre, and COPPER MINES at the sides, this stamp was printed from electrotypes made from a woodblock original.

A rival company called the Great Barrier Pigeongram Agency was formed in the spring of 1899. Originally it levied a charge of 2s per message but soon reduced this in face of competition from the original company and when it was discovered that a pigeon was capable of carrying four messages instead of one. The revised rate was 6d per message to Auckland and a shilling for the return journey. In July 1899 triangular 6d blue and 1s red stamps were lithographed at Auckland. The central motif showed a pigeon in flight and the three side panels were inscribed GREAT BARRIER ISLD—PIGEON GRAM—AUCKLAND. Generally speaking used examples of the pigeon post stamps of New Zealand are scarcer than mint, while stamps still affixed to the original flimsies are of considerable rarity. Even rarer are examples of the special envelopes into which the flimsies were placed for delivery to the recipient. In 1949 the Air Mail Society of New Zealand commemorated the golden jubilee of the Great Barrier Island services by producing attractive facsimiles of the 6d triangular stamp in blue and gold.

An efficient pigeon post service was organised in Ceylon in the 1850s by the proprietors of the *Ceylon Observer* between the mail steamer port of Galle and the capital, Colombo. The service was instituted primarily to expedite news of the Crimean War and the distance covered was 72 miles. It was discontinued in 1858 when the telegraph service was extended from Colombo to Galle Point. Specially prepared despatches from the fortnightly or monthly mail steamers were made up at Galle and transmitted by pigeons who made the flight in about an hour. Although this service was terminated on the advent of the telegraph there is in the Fitzgerald Collection at the British Museum a tiny four page newspaper, entitled *Home News* and dated London 10 June 1873, with each page stamped at the foot PER CARRIER PIGEON in pale grey lettering. This is the earliest recorded use of a special cachet on pigeon mail.

The use of pigeons for semi-official postal services in India itself came much later but was a popular method for publicity purposes in the 1930s. The first of these pigeon mail flights took place in February 1931 between Asansol and Calcutta, a distance of 132 miles. The flimsies were rolled up and inserted in aluminium containers attached to the bird's leg. Pigeons carried from two to eight flimsies in this way. When the birds alighted in Calcutta the flimsies were detached, unrolled and placed in special envelopes bearing a cachet FIRST INDIAN PIGEONGRAM with a picture of a pigeon above. This service was carried out to commemorate the 20th anniversary of the world's first official airmail by heavier-than-air machine—the Allahabad flight of February 1911. Special message forms were printed by the Calcutta Homing Pigeon Club which organised the flight.

Later flights were organised as propaganda for the Viceroy's annual New Year's message. The first of the Viceroy flights, organised by the Indian Air Mail Society and the Calcutta Homing Pigeon Club, took place on 31 December 1931. The printed flimsy on this occasion bore the legend PIGEONGRAM— A MESSAGE FOR 1932 FROM HIS EXCELLENCY THE VICEROY— HONESTY IS THE BEST POLICY. Details of the flight, from Hazaribagh to Calcutta, and the name of the pigeon in each case, were given below. The flimsies on arrival at Calcutta were put in specially printed envelopes which also included space for the pigeon's name to be inserted in manuscript. The covers were then despatched to the addressee in the normal way. The postal authorities took note of the special occasion by allowing a red, instead of black, postmark to be used to cancel the adhesive stamps. On 11 January 1933 the Viceroy, Lord Willingdon, sent a goodwill message from his camp to the Indian Air Mail Society. The flimsies were carried by a relay of birds from the Calcutta Homing Pigeon Club. The flimsies were placed in small envelopes to which were affixed specially printed labels showing a pigeon superimposed on a map of India with the Union Jack at the top. The inscription on the label read A MESSAGE FROM HE THE VICEROY. A few labels are known with the misspelling MASSAGE for MESSAGE.

Further pigeon despatches for which special flimsies, covers or labels were produced appeared in October 1933 (Puri to Calcutta), in October 1940 (a Red Cross charity flight from Chandernagore to Calcutta) and in April 1941 (from Kalayan to Bombay). On the last of these flights 250 carrier pigeons of the Royal Indian Navy were used as a means of raising funds for the Royal Indian Navy War Purposes Fund. The printed message from Sir Roger Lumley, Governor of Bombay, to Vice-

Admiral Fitzherbert of the Royal Indian Navy, was placed in special blue envelopes with a large pigeon outlined in white. On this occasion the postal authorities sanctioned a special red wavy-line cancellation inscribed KALAYAN—FIRST PIGEON MISSIVE, with the date 6 APR. 1941 in the centre. These covers were subsequently sold to the general public for 2 rupees.

Special flimsies with the heading H M NAVAL PIGEON SERVICE were supplied to members of the British Auxiliary Volunteer Service between 1896 and 1903 for use in naval emergencies. According to the 'Aero Field' Handbook *British Air Mails 1784-1946*, two unused flimsies have been recorded but no flown examples. The service was finally discontinued in 1907 when all extant material was destroyed. Homing pigeons were used for the dissemination of propaganda material in connection with various fund-raising schemes during the First World War and, of course, pigeons were used extensively by the British Army in France, special flimsies inscribed ROYAL AIR FORCE PIGEON SERVICE being used at the end of the war.

Pigeon posts were organised on infrequent occasions in the years between the World Wars, mainly to raise funds for charities. In this category come the Sandringham-London flight of November 1924, in connection with a London Hospital appeal, the Grace Darling commemorative flight from Battersea Park, London in November 1934 and the Silver Jubilee flight at Edinburgh in May 1935. A pigeon post service was also organised in June 1939 during salvage operations connected with the submarine *Thetis* and the following month pigeons were used to despatch miniature editions of the *Dunlop Gazette* from Fort Dunlop (Birmingham) to Coventry. The pigeon post service was used extensively during the Second World War, mainly in connection with fund-raising schemes, as during the First World War, and since 1945 there have been sporadic examples of pigeongrams, mostly of a charitable or philatelic nature. The only other example of a pigeon post service of note in the British Isles was operated between Herm and Guernsey in the Channel Islands in 1949. Special 1s adhesive stamps, depicting a pigeon in flight with a letter attached to its feet, were produced, but the service, inaugurated on 26 May 1949, seems to have been shortlived. Examples of this pigeongram stamp on flown flimsies are of great interest to collectors.

Many other countries have produced examples of a pigeon post at some time or other, but in every instance it has been a case of fund-raising, propaganda or publicity stunt rather than dictated by necessity. The development of telegraphic communication, and the overall improvement in other methods of aerial or surface communications, have rendered the pigeon post valueless except as an occasional gimmick.

In July 1905 the French newspaper *Le Matin* organised a pigeon post to demonstrate the usefulness of this medium. Birds were released from Paris in the direction of St Quentin or Amiens, carrying flimsies which were placed in special envelopes attached to the fronts of special postcards and mailed to the recipient in the normal way. In addition pigeons bearing these flimsies were released from the steamer *Ariane*, off the Cornish coast near Penzance. Some 5,000 of these flimsies and postcards were presented to subscribers to the newspaper but surprisingly few of them seem to have been preserved and are now rated among the most expensive of French airmail souvenirs

Glider Posts

Bearing in mind the fact that gliders had been developed to a comparative degree of sophistication in the decades before powered flight it is, perhaps, surprising that greater use was not made of this medium for the carriage of airmail. But the principal drawback about gliders is the fact that, like free balloons, they must go whither wind and air current dictate. Thus they could only be used either as a last resort in times of emergency, or for non-essential purposes, for publicity at fairs and exhibitions, or on sporting events.

Otto and Gustav Lilienthal began experimenting with gliders as long ago as 1867, but only achieved manned glider flights in 1891. Otto was killed in a gliding accident five years later: his memory was perpetuated in one of Germany's two high-value airmail stamps of 1934, Count Zeppelin being portrayed on the other. Nevertheless the Lilienthal brothers laid the foundations for gliding which was to become a very popular sport in Germany, especially after the First World War when the development of powered aircraft was severely restricted by the terms of the Treaty of Versailles. Furthermore the meteorological conditions prevailing in the Rhine Valley favoured gliding, and as a result Germany and Austria dominated the international gliding scene in the years between the wars. The sport spread rapidly to other countries and became popular in Russia, Britain and the United States. Gliders were used with devastating effect by the Germans in the invasion of the Low Countries in 1940 and Crete in 1941 for the assault of these areas by airborne troops, and the same techniques were applied by the Allies on D-Day and at Arnhem in 1944.

A surprising amount of mail has been flown by glider since 1923 when Austria, Britain and Germany produced glider mail flights almost simultaneously. At the end of August 1923 a Glider Meeting was held at Gersfeld in the Rhineland and obsolete German airmail stamps (1919 series) were unofficially over-printed ERSTER POST SEGELFLUG 1923 (First Glider Flight Post). In the ensuing years glider meetings were held regularly at Gersfeld, Pforzheim and Riesengebirge and special labels, semi-official stamps, stationery and postmarks were produced in pro-fusion. Britain's one and only glider post occurred in October 1923 when the *Daily Mail* offered a prize of £1,000 for the longest distance accomplished in one flight by motor-assisted gliders using one gallon of fuel. The competition was held at Lympne and the prize was divided between the English Electric Company and the Air Navigation and Engineering Company. The latter carried a small quantity of mail from Lympne to Hastingleigh on 13 October, the last day of the meeting, the letters being handed over to the Post Office on landing. Special covers and labels were used, the latter being inscribed CARRIED BY MOTOR GLIDER FROM LYMPNE TO HASTINGLEIGH. Austria's first glider post appeared on 19 October 1923 when a special cancel-lation was applied to mail at the Glider Meeting held at Wasch-berg bei Stockeran. Ten years elapsed before Austria's next glider mails. In January 1933 a Glider Exhibition was staged in Vienna, organised by Robert Kronfeld, an Austrian who later became a naturalised Briton and served with great distinction in the RAF throughout the Second World War. In May 1933 mail was flown by glider between Graz in Austria and Maribor in Yugoslavia and large cachets were struck on souvenir cards and covers.

During the Second World War effective use was made of trans-port gliders towed by a powered aircraft. In this way vast numbers of troops and their equipment were ferried across the English Channel to the Normandy landings in 1944. The idea of using an aeroplane to tow a string of gliders was not new, however, and as early as 1930 a glider had been towed across the United States from San Diego, California, to New York. Four years later an aeroplane towing three gliders, known as the Lustig Sky Train, flew successfully from New York to Washington. One of the glider pilots in this case, Jack O'Meara, organised a Glider Train to Cuba in 1935, carrying mail by this means from Havana to Miami. The Cuban authorities issued the 10c air stamp with an overprint PRIMER TREN AEREO INTERNACIONAL 1935 (First International Air Train) with the names of the organisers, O'Meara and Du Pont.

Since the Second World War gliders have been used to carry mail at aviation meetings, sporting events, exhibitions and fairs in several countries; Holland, Great Britain, Liechtenstein and Poland among others, but the strongest interest in this field remains in Austria and Germany where gliding is as popular a sport as it was in the prewar years.

Balloon Posts

The development of dirigible airships in the early years of this century did away with the utilitarian purposes to which free balloons could be applied. With the exception of the siege of Przemysl already referred to there was no occasion in the twentieth century in which free balloons had a serious purpose. Freed from the dictates of practicability the free balloon made something of a come-back as a purely sporting medium of transport and, indeed, even in these days of supersonic air-liners and space travel, ballooning is becoming more and more fashionable as a sport.

The sporting element in free ballooning was stimulated in the years before the Second World War by the annual balloon races sponsored by the American newspaper proprietor, James Gordon-Bennett II. The sponsor donated a valuable trophy to be awarded to the pilot of the balloon which travelled farthest from the starting point, the time taken being immaterial. The country of the winner was to undertake to hold the race the following year. The first of these International Free Balloon Races was staged near Paris, France, on 30 June 1906 and races were held in subsequent years in the United States (1907, 1910 and 1911), Germany (1908 and 1912), Switzerland (1909) and France 1913. No races were held until 1920 when the United States was again the host country. From then until 1938 the Gordon-Bennett Races, as they were popularly known, were held annually: in Belgium (1921, 1923-6 and 1937-8), Switzerland (1922 and 1932), the United States (1927-30 and 1932) and Poland (1934-6). Poland was to have been host to the 1939 race but this was cancelled on account of the outbreak of the Second World War and the races were not revived after the war. No race took place in 1931 since the proposed host country, the United States, was hard hit by the Depression at the time.

Souvenir mails were carried on many of the balloons taking part in these races. The only country to issue stamps in honour of the race was Poland which in 1936 overprinted two stamps GORDON-BENNETT 30. VIII. 1936. Poland also produced several semi-official sets of balloon mail stamps, in 1926 and 1928 for national balloon competitions, and then in 1939, a set of three in honour of the Gordon-Bennett race of that year. The 1939 race having been cancelled these stamps were never put to postal use and are regarded more as fund-raising labels. However, 1,700 postcards bearing sets of the stamps were posted in Brussels on 31 August 1939. It was intended that these cards would be carried by the Belgian balloon piloted by E. Demuyter. A few of these cards are known with a blue cachet inscribed in Polish GORDON-BENNETT CUP, LWOW, 3.9.1939—CANCELLED BECAUSE OF THE WAR.

Flown covers and postcards from the Gordon-Bennett balloon races have been recorded from 1909 onwards. Special postmarks and cachets were often applied to mail at the starting point of the race, and postmarks of the place of descent added on arrival, sometimes with the stamps of the country concerned affixed for good measure. Publicity stickers and fund-raising labels were produced for many of the races from 1912 onwards and postcards depicting the ascent of the balloons exist as far back as the Paris race of 1906.

Although the Gordon-Bennett Cup races were not revived after the Second World War ballooning as such has steadily gained in popularity. Races, exhibitions and other flights by free balloon have taken place in many countries since the war and since souvenir postcards and covers were carried on most occasions the scope for the collector is immense. A number of flights have been made in connection with the Alfred Leblanc Prize for long-distance balloon flights. The first of these races took place at Le Mans in May 1947 and special labels and cachets were produced in honour of the event.

The first postwar balloon post in Germany was organised in

May 1949, the starting-point being Berg Neustadt. Again special cachets and covers were prepared and the postal authorities provided a pictorial postmark. Germany, Austria and the Netherlands have produced many examples of balloon posts in the past 20 years. Historic balloon ascents have themselves been commemorated by special stamps and postmarks and, in some cases, balloon posts have been organised as part of the commemoration. In this category come the cancellations and cachets marking the 175th anniversary of the first Dutch ascent (1955), the centenary of John Wise and the *Jupiter* flight (1959) and the French *Journée du Timbre* (Day of the Stamp) which, in 1955, chose the Paris balloon mail as its theme.

More than anyone else Dr Jan Boesman of the Netherlands has been responsible for stimulating postwar interest in ballooning as a sport and he has made numerous ascents, often with his wife Nini as co-pilot, in recent years in countries as far afield as the United States and Bulgaria. An aerophilatelist of international repute and an authority on the history of ballooning and balloon posts, Dr Boesman has ensured that the balloon flights with which he has been associated are well documented with souvenir cards, covers, postmarks and cachets. The supreme accolade was paid him by Haiti in November 1968. In connection with a balloon flight which he made in Haiti that country issued two stamps depicting his balloon and bearing his portrait inset—an honour which is given to few aeronauts in their lifetime.

Helicopter Mail

Ever since Leonardo da Vinci produced his ideas for a flying machine man has sought ways of inventing a flying machine on the rotating wing principle. Although the first heavier-than-air machines were designed with fixed wings the idea of rotating blades as the source of lift was not abandoned. In 1907 Louis Breguet built the first successful helicopter but its inherent instability made it impracticable. Almost 30 years later, Breguet perfected this machine and paved the way for the Russian-born Igor Sikorsky to make it a practical proposition.

In the interim both David Kay in Scotland and Juan de la Cierva in Spain designed autogyros, aircraft powered by propellers in the usual way but given added stability by means of rotary instead of fixed wings. These wings rotated freely in the air current set up by the forward movement of the aircraft and thus the autogyro lacked the advantages of the helicopter. Autogyros enjoyed a measure of popularity in the 1930s but their practicability was limited and they were eventually superseded by the helicopter itself. Nevertheless examples of mail carried by autogyro are recorded. An autogyro was used to fly mail from Hanworth to Windsor in connection with APEX, the international airpost exhibition in May 1934 and special labels were used in addition to the APEX cachet and postmark. The same autogyro carried souvenir mail from Melbourne to Portland during the Victoria Centenary celebrations in November 1934. Four years later an autogyro service by Eastern Air Lines was operated between Philadelphia Post Office and Camden airfield in order to expedite the mails.

The advent of the Second World War prevented the further development of autogyros and in the postwar period the helicopter emerged as the answer to short flights between towns where elaborate landing facilities were not required. In July 1946 the first helicopter mail was flown in Los Angeles by personnel of Air Transport Command and the Air Rescue Service. A special cachet featuring a Sikorsky helicopter and inscribed U S AIR MAIL LOS ANGELES AREA EXPERIMENTAL HELICOPTER SERVICE OPERATED BY ARMY AIR FORCES was applied to flown covers. Three routes with almost 40 stopping places were involved. In October 1946 a similar service, with 43 alighting points on four routes, commenced in the Chicago area and again a large pictorial cachet was employed on flown mail. In January 1947 a service began in New York; again a colourful cachet was applied to flown items. These experiments having proved successful, the Los Angeles service was put on a regular footing in October 1947 and similar services were gradually introduced throughout the United States in the ensuing years.

The first helicopter mail flights in Europe took place in 1947. On 5 November mail was flown from The Hague to Brussels and return by helicopter and a special pictorial postmark was used to celebrate the occasion. In February of that year mail was flown by helicopter from HMS *Vanguard* to Portsmouth at the beginning of the Royal Tour to South Africa. Mail for the Royal Family was also carried by helicopter in August 1947 between Dyce Airport and Balmoral Castle in Aberdeenshire. Neither occasion, however, resulted in philatelic material available to collectors. In February 1948 a helicopter was used in an emergency to take mail to and from the Wolf Rock lighthouse when it was cut off for several weeks by stormy weather, and a few souvenir covers were carried 'by favour'.

Experimental helicopter flights were made by BEA in the spring and summer of 1948 in the west country and East Anglia. Though no mail was carried on these trial flights it was as a result of their success that a twice-daily helicopter mail service was inaugurated on 1 June 1948 in East Anglia, the route with 14 calling points covering 102 miles. Special envelopes and pictorial cachets were produced in connection with the inaugural flight. Helicopter mail, under the Air Letter service, was flown regularly between London and Birmingham from November 1953 onwards. In 1961 BEA produced a special helicopter stamp, for use on mail flown by this method between London and Windsor to commemorate the golden jubilee of the first British official airmail, the Coronation Aerial Post of 1911.

In Europe itself Sweden has operated helicopter flights in emergency during the winter months from 1948 onwards for the relief of the offshore islands when sea communication is impossible on account of frozen conditions. In the same year the first Swiss helipost came into operation, with mail flights between the airport and main post office in Zurich. Two years later, on 2 October 1950, a helicopter flight organised by the Italian and Swiss Aero Clubs was made from Brig in Switzerland to Domodossola, to mark the 50th anniversary of the death of Jorge Chavez (see Chapter 4). Mail was carried by a Bell 47 D1 helicopter of Aersilta, Milan and marked with a souvenir cachet inscribed in English, German and Italian.

In the 1950s the use of helicopters for regular mail flights increased in Europe. Sabena began their Belgian service in August 1950 with a 270-mile circuit covering ten cities and towns. In 1953 Sabena introduced an international helicopter service with mail flights from Brussels to Rotterdam (Holland), Lille (France) and Cologne and Bonn (Germany). Special covers, cards, cachets and postmarks were used for the inaugural flights in each case. In addition helicopter flights have become a popular feature at exhibitions, philatelic and otherwise, and the souvenir mail from such occasions augments the interest of a collection devoted to this facet of aerophilately. In July-August 1952 two USAF Sikorsky S.55 helicopters made the first trans-Atlantic flight, from East Hertford, Connecticut to West Germany, via Goose Bay (Labrador), Narsarssuck (Greenland),

Keflavik (Iceland) and Prestwick (Scotland). A small quantity of covers was carried and postmarked at the United States Army Post Office on 6 August on arrival in Germany. In more recent years there have been special helicopter mail flights from the ships involved in the recovery of space capsules in the Apollo programme. Covers bearing colourful cachets and the ships' postmarks add a new dimension to helicopter airmail and link it with man's greatest achievements in aviation to date.

Rocket Posts

Experiments with mail-carrying rockets began in Austria in 1928 when Friedrich Schmiedl carried out tests with his V series of projectiles. Apart from personal messages no mail was flown by Schmiedl's rockets until February 1931 when the V-7 was successfully launched. Later in the same year Schmiedl despatched mails by other rockets, including the R-1 on which mail from the general public was launched. Throughout 1932 and 1933 Schmiedl's experiments developed and the projectiles were numbered progressively up to V-16 and by December of the latter year had even launched two-stage rockets. When the first stage was exhausted it floated to earth by means of a parachute. Souvenir mail was housed in each of the two stages flown. In 1935, after a gap of 14 months, he embarked on the N series of rockets. These missiles numbered N1 to 9 all carried small quantities of mail, the last of these flights being made in Yugoslavia. Special covers and cachets, often including Schmiedl's autograph, were produced for all of these flights. Special rocket stamps were used on mail flown by R-1, V9 and some other missiles.

The first rocket flight carrying mail was made in Germany in April 1931 by Reinhold Tiling: 188 postcards were launched on that occasion. Tiling was killed soon afterwards as the result of a rocket explosion and it was left to Gerhard Zucker to continue rocket mail experiments in the 1930s. Zucker made his first rocket flight in April 1933 at Duhnen on the North Sea coast. Later flights were made in the Harz Mountains and in January 1934 special stamps were applied to rocket covers organised by Zucker to raise funds for the Nazi Winter Relief Fund.

In the summer of 1934 Zucker came to England to attend the international airpost exhibition (APEX) in London. A rocket mail flight was to have taken place in connection with the exhibition but it had to be postponed. Special triangular stamps, however, were prepared in this connection, but were subsequently used for rocket flights in the Netherlands. Zucker's first rocket mail flight in Britain took place in June 1934 at Rottingdean on the Sussex Downs. APEX souvenir labels with a special overprint were used on covers and cards flown by rocket on this occasion. At the end of July Zucker moved to the Outer Hebrides where he attempted to send mail by rocket from the island of Scarp to the island of Harris. Trouble with the fuel used on this occasion culminated in the explosion of the rocket on the beach on take-off. Many of the covers were slightly charred by the explosion and were subsequently endorsed with a three-line cachet by the postmaster of Harris. Special stamps, in denominations of 2s 6d and 5s, inscribed WESTERN ISLES ROCKET POST were produced on this occasion. Later these stamps were overprinted for use on mail carried by rocket in attempts between Lymington, Hampshire, and the Isle of Wight. These experiments also were doomed to failure. Zucker subsequently conducted rocket experiments in Belgium, Holland, Switzerland and other European countries. After 1934, however, the Nazis imposed a ban on Zucker's work and henceforward rocket research in Germany was concentrated on the military aspects, leading eventually to the V1 and V2 guided weapons of the Second World War.

Curiously enough the country which produced the greatest number of rocket mail flights before the Second World War was India, where Dr Stephen Smith conducted experiments between September 1934 and December 1944. In that period Dr Smith launched no fewer than 59 mail-carrying rockets in India and made another 16 rocket flights between April and October 1935 alone, in connection with the Sikkim Durbar of that year. Special rocket stamps, labels, cards and covers were produced for these flights.

Since the Second World War rocket mail experiments have been continued and are now in progress in many countries under the auspices of bodies such as the Paisley Rocketeers in Scotland and SOAR (the Society of Applied Rocketry) in the United States. While the majority of these flights are in the nature of stunts organised in connection with exhibitions the time may not be far off when rockets will be used for the transportation of mail on a serious basis. Already philately has found its way to the moon, by means of manned space-ship. At the time of the Apollo 11 moonlanding in 1969 the astronauts took with them the die for a postage stamp actually showing them setting foot on the moon's surface. When the lunar module touched down on the moon the astronauts pulled an impression of this die on paper, thus creating the moon's first postage stamp. This die was later returned to earth, decontaminated, and then used in the manufacture of the printing plate for America's 10 cents airmail stamp issued in September 1969. The astronauts also took to the moon an envelope franked with an imperforate coloured die proof of the stamp. This they cancelled on the moon with a special postmark inscribed MOON LANDING USA with the date JUL 20 1969 in the centre. The first lunar post office operated with a minimum of equipment—one rubber stamp and an ink-pad. The three astronauts later described how they stacked hands on the hand-stamp and together postmarked the first piece of moon mail. Although the mail on which the 10c stamp at present prepays postage is of a more mundane, terrestrial nature, we can no doubt look forward, in the second century of airmails, to the development of inter-planetary mail flights and at last the rocket, regarded at the moment as no more than a gimmick in aerophilately, will come into its own.

13

Bibliography

1. CATALOGUES

Baldwin, N. C., *Great Britain and Ireland: a catalogue of internal airmails, 1910-1941* (1942)
Boesman, Nini, *World Catalogue of Balloonposts* (1968)
Champion, Theodore, *Catalogue Historique et Descriptif des Timbres de la Poste Aerienne* (various editions since 1921)
Curtis, C. J., *Catalogue of Forces Covers* (1955-6)
Field, David, *Priced Catalogue of Airmail Stamps and Airposts of the World* (1934)
Gibbons, Stanley Ltd, *Catalogue of air stamps* (1937)
Godinas, F., *World's Air Mail Catalogue of Aerogrammes and Postal Stationery* (1955)
Horton-Smith, D. A. G., *Mussons' airmail catalogue. Part 1. Europe* (1946)
Kessler, F. W., *Aerogramme Catalogue* (1961-63)
Melville, F. J., *Aero stamps. A descriptive catalogue with prices* (1920)
Morgan, Ian C., *Specialised Air Stamp Catalogue of Canada* (1934-5)
Sanabria, Nicolas, *The World Airmail Catalog* (1966); *The World Airmail News* (supplements to the Catalog)
Sieger, Verlag, *Katalog der Flugpost de Neuen Deutschen Lufthansa* (various editions); *Zeppelin Post Catalogue* (various edtions); *German Airpost Catalogue* (various editions); *Austrian Airpost Catalogue* (various editions)
Silombra, Jean, *Catalogue de la Poste Aerienne* (various editions)
Stephen, J., *Airgraph and V mail catalogue, 1948* (1948)
Tocila, M., *Luchtpost Catalogue van Nederland en de Overzeese Gebiedsdelen* (1948-55)

2. HANDBOOKS

Airmail Society of New Zealand, *The Internal Air Mails of New Zealand* (1955)

Armstrong, Douglas B., *Romance of the air post. An introduction to air post collecting* (1926)

Auckland, R. G., *Aerial propaganda leaflets dropped by the R.A.F. in the Far East between 1942-1945* (1957)

Auckland, R. G., *A checklist of German propaganda leaflets airdropped to British and American troops between October 1944-March 1945* (1957)

Baker, E. C., *Airgraph service 1941-1945* (1953)

Baldwin, N. C., *Air mail digest 1-10: British Commonwealth* (1954); *Air mail labels (Etiquettes)* (1940); *Air mails of Bermuda* (1967); *Airmails of British Africa 1925-1932* (1932); *Arctic airmails* (1966); *Bridging the Atlantic* (1951); *British airmails. A chronology of the air posts of Great Britain and Ireland* (1935); *British airmails 1784-1946* (1952); *British airmails 1946-1951. An illustrated and priced supplement to British airmails 1784-1946* (1951); *Deutsche Lufthansa and Lufthansa* (1966); *External airmails of Australia* (1966); *Fifty years of British airmails, 1911-1960* (1961); *First British airway letter stamps; Imperial Airways: a history and priced check list of the Empire airmails* (1950); *Portuguese Africa. The Special Status air stamps* (1949); *Post war bridging the Atlantic, 1945-1950* (1952); *World air posts* (1948)

Bentley, Rev. Wilfrid, *Postal History and Postmarks of the Franco-Prussian War* (1955)

Bigsby, G. H., *Price list and guide to collecting of Paris Siege Balloon Post 1870-1871* (1928)

Boesman, Jan, *40 years of K.L.M. Post Fights; Ballon Aventuren* (1961)

Clement, Alfred, *Handbuch der Militär-Luftpost, 1793-1953*

Cohen, E. M., *The 1870 Paris Siege Balloons* (1970)

Collins, R. J. G., *The Air Mails and Pigeon Posts of New Zealand* (1931)

Crome, E. A., *Quantas Aeriana, 1920-1954* (1955)

Dalwick, R. E. R. and Harmer, C. H. C.. *Newfoundland airmails, 1919-1939* (1953)

Davey, C. J., *Indian airmail* (1948)

Davis, Alec, *Aircraft spotting in cachets*

Fawdry, C. W., *The airposts in Siam, 1919-1935* (1936)
Field, Francis J., *British Empire. First special mail flights, summary of historical airmails of 52 countries* (1932); *British inland airposts, 1934: first official airmail flight 20th & 21st* (1934); *The Coronation aerial post, 1911* (1934)
Field, John C. W., *Aerial propaganda leaflets: a collectors handbook* (1954); *Bridging the Pacific: a priced chronology of projected, attempted and successful Pacific flights from 1919-1951* (1951); *Japan: overseas and international flights* (1959); *Palestine and Israel*
Fitzgerald, Mrs A., *Notebook of an amateur collector of early souvenirs of the airpost* (1950); *The notebook of an amateur collector of early souvenirs of the air post. France; The notebook of an amateur collector of early souvenirs of the air post. Italy*
Francois, L., *Les Correspondances par Ballon monté du Siège de Paris* (1925)
Fresson, E. E., *Air Road to the Isles* (1967)
Gebauer, E., *The Air Post of Colombia*
General Post Office, *Airmail services, Imperial and foreign* (1947); *Letter airmails. European countries* (1934)
Gisburn, H. G. D., *The air mail of New Guinea* (1950); *An airmail pioneer* (1949); *Thirty years of K.L.M.* (1949)
Glines, C. V., *The saga of the airmail* (1968)
Harper, H. and Brenard, R., *The romance of the flying mail: a pageant of aerial progress* (1933)
Harris, L. H., *World's first air stamps: Italy 1917* (1959)
Heyd, Gunther, *Paris par Moulins* (1970)
Hill, R. H., *The Baghdad airmail* (1929)
Hopkins, A. E., *A pioneer of British airmail, Bath-London* (1929)
Hughes, W. E., *Chronicles of Icarus No. 2. Airmails of Great Britain* (1930); *Stamps of the flying post* (1922)
Imperial Airways Ltd, *Empire airmail: inauguration* (1938)
Kessler, F. W., *Airposts of Colombia* (1936)
Levi-Castillo, Dr Eduardo, *SCADTA Airmails of Ecuador* (1961)
Loening, Grover, *Fifty Years of Flying Progress* (1955)
Lumley, D. O., *Airmail* (1939)
Mackay, James A., *One Hundred Leaves: Notes on the Fitzgerald Airmail Collection* (1964)
Maincent, Paul, *Genèse de la Poste Aérienne du Siège de Paris* (1951)
Mallet, F., *Les Aeronautes et les Colombophiles du Siège de*

Paris (1909)
Mann, Jason T. W., *Great Britain. The postmarks and envelopes of the airgraph service, May 1941-August 1945*
Melville, Frederick J., *Aero Stamp collecting* (1924)
Monk, E. V. and Winter, H. T., *Airmail* (1936)
Nadar, *Les Ballons en 1870* (1870)
Newport, William, *Airmails of the Channel Islands* (1957)
Nielson, Dale, *Saga of the U.S. Airmail Service* (1963)
Phillips, A., *British inland airmails, April 1933-1935, from 'dawn to the awakening'* (1935)
Phillips, Harold D., *Civil Aviation* (1943)
Philips, Stanley, *By air through the stamp album* (1934)
Pringle, John, *Early balloon posts* (1936)
Redgrave, H. Stanley, *The airmails of the British Isles* (1940)
Ridgeway, Brig. Gen. R., *Airpost stamps* (1922)
Roadcap, R. R., *World Airline Record* (various editions)
Scott, H. Eric, *The Daily Mail Tours of Great Britain, 1912* (1970)
Smith, Col. L. H., *The Ross Smith England-Australia Flight* (1968)
Smith, John A., *The history of the R.A.F. postal service overseas, 1942-1957* (1957)
Smith, K. Stewart, *Airgraph service: May 1941-August 1945, a short account* (1946)
Stephen, J., *Zeppelin transatlantic record flight and air race cover price list* (1948)
Stern, Capt. M. F., *South African Air Mails*
Thorsteinsson, S., *Icelandic Air Mails* (1970)
Walker, J. Reg., *New Zealand: The Great Barrier Island 1898-99 Pigeon Post Stamps* (1968)
Webb, F. J., *Hong Kong Airmails* (1968)
White, John Baker *The Big Lie* (1956) (an American history of propaganda leaflets)
Williams, L. N. and M., *Airmail collectors notebook* (1960)
Williamson, Sir F. H., *The airmail service* (1934)

3. PERIODICALS

Aerial Messenger (journal of the Aero Philatelic Club, London)
The Aero Field (Sutton Coldfield, England)
Aero Philatelists Annals, edited by the late Henry Goodkind, New York

Airmail Digest Year-Book, various editions, edited by Ernest
A. Kehr (Now York)

The Airmail Entire Truth (bulletin of the International Study
Group for Aerogrammes, New York)

Airmail News (bi-montly organ of the British Air Mail Society,
London)

The Airpost Journal (American Airmail Society, New York)

The Falling Leaf (journal of the Psywar [Psychological Warfare]
Society) Kettering, Northants

Luftpost Nachrichten (journal of Central Commission for
Philately, Deutscher Kulturbund, Jena, German Democratic
Republic)

14

Index